English
for Junior Certificate
Ordinary Level

LESS STRESS MORE SUCCESS

English for Junior Certificate Ordinary Level

Louise O'Reilly

Gill & Macmillan

Gill & Macmillan Ltd
Hume Avenue
Park West
Dublin 12
with associated companies throughout the world
www.gillmacmillan.ie

© Louise O'Reilly, 2007

978 0 7171 4231 6

Colour reproduction by Typeform Repro, Dublin
Print origination in Ireland by Carole Lynch

The paper used in this book is made from the wood pulp of managed forests. For every tree felled, at least one tree is planted, thereby renewing natural resources.

For permission to reproduce photographs the author and publisher gratefully acknowledge the following:

59, 60, 61 © The Advertising Archives; 33, 34B, 79 © Alamy;
71, 72 © Camera Press; 22 Image © Burstein Collection/Corbis
Artwork © The Munch Museum/The Munch-Ellingsen Group;
66, 67, 68, 69 Courtesy of Irish Water Safety, the statutory voluntary body established to promote water safety in Ireland; 63 © Martyn Turner;
54, 65 © Reuters; 80T © Rex Features; 80B © Topfoto.

CONTENTS

ACKNOWLEDGMENTS

For permission to reproduce copyright material in this book, grateful acknowledgment is made to the following:

'Sink Eating' by Peter Cunningham. Peter Cunningham is a novelist and living in Ireland; 'A Mysterious Lady' by Michael Cox, Scholastic Ltd; 'Jumping for Joy' from *Ireland's Friendly Dolphin* by Sean Mannion, Brandon Books; *Fly, Cherokee, Fly*, copyright Chris d'Lacey, Transworld 1998; 222 words from *Of Mice and Men* by John Steinbeck (Penguin, 2000). Copyright © John Steinbeck, 1937, 1965. Reproduced by permission of Penguin Books Ltd; adapted extract from *Life of Pi* © Yann Martel, Cannongate Books; extract from *Pirates* © Celia Rees, Bloomsbury, 2003; 84 words from *The Wish List* by Eoin Colfer (Puffin, 2002). Copyright © Eoin Colfer, 2002. Reproduced by permission of Penguin Books Ltd; *The Irish Times* for 'Online Shopping' by Chris Johns; A & C Black publishers for the extracts from *Our Day Out* and *Blood Brothers* by Willy Russell; *The Irish Times* for the review 'Mission Impossible III' by Michael Dwyer; extract from *Lovers* (*Winners and Losers*) (1984) by Brian Friel by kind permission of the author and The Gallery Press, Loughcrew, Oldcastle, County Meath, Ireland; extract from *Just the Job* by Ann Farquhar-Smith © Ann Farquhar-Smith; Michigan State University Press for 'An African Thunderstorm' by David Rubadiri; 'The Old Lady' by Robert Adcock; 'Visitor' by Wes Magee, Penguin Books Ltd; 'Mid Term Break' & 'The Early Purges' by Seamus Heaney, Faber and Faber; 'Dulce et Decorum Est' by Wilfred Owen, Faber and Faber; The Literary Trustees of Walter de la Mare and the Society of Authors as their representative for the poem 'The Listeners' by Walter de la Mare; 'Fight!' by Barrie Wade, Collins Educational; 'In My Life', words & music by John Lennon & Paul McCartney © Copyright 1965 Northern Songs. Used by permission of Music Sales Limited. All Rights Reserved. International Copyright Secured; adapted extract 'Walter's Story' from *Mr Vertigo* by Paul Auster, Penguin Books Ltd; adapted extract from 'Thank You Ma'am' by Langston Hughes, Random House; 'The Sniper' from *Liam O'Flaherty: Short Stories*, Wolfhound Press, 1996, © Liam O' Flaherty PFD Agency; 'My First Confession' approximately 3,395 words (pp. 43-51) from *My Oedipus Complex and Other Stories* by Frank O'Connor (Penguin Books, 1963, 2001). Copyright © Frank O'Connor; 'The Highest Place on Earth' (adapted) by Pat Falvey from *The Quiet Quarter Anthology of New Irish Writing*, Edited by Eoin Brady, New Island Books; 'Life Story' (adapted) by Frank O'Hara, Random House; extract from *SWALK: Collection of Short Stories* by Sam McBratney, Collins; The Agency for an adapted scene from *Kes* by Barry Hines and Allan Stronach.

Some extracts were adapted by the State Examinations Commission exclusively for the purposes of the Junior Certificate English (Ordinary Level) examination papers and do not purport to be the authors' original published texts.

The Exam

The Junior Certificate English exam is a two and a half hour exam divided into seven sections. You have approximately 25 minutes per section.

Sections 1, 2, 3 and 4 are compulsory and therefore must be answered. Sections 5, 6 and 7 vary in topic, but you have to answer any two of these three sections. This means that whatever topic is in section 4, either Poetry, Fiction, Drama or Media Studies, **must** be answered. In sections 5, 6 and 7, you have the option of leaving out one section.

Your timetable for the exam breaks down like this:

9.30	Section 1	Reading section
9.55	Section 2	Personal writing (essay)
10.20	Section 3	Functional writing
10.45	Section 4 (Must do)	Poetry
11.05	Section 5/6/7	Drama
11.30	Section 5/6/7	Fiction
		Media studies
11.55	Check work	
12.00	Finish	

It is very important that you stick to allowing yourself only 25 minutes for each section. Each section carries 60 marks and you will be doing yourself no favours by spending an hour finishing off that thrilling four-page essay and leaving out all of a later section!

It is up to you to move on to the next section as soon as your 25 minutes are up. Come back to an earlier section at the end if you have time. You cannot be given marks for blank sections, so don't throw away your marks.

KEY WORDS

There are certain words that are used in the questions in the exam. It is your responsibility to make sure you understand the typical vocabulary of the exam questions. The following examples are used regularly in the exam:

- **Composition:** This means your essay or story.
- **Convey:** To show or express. You may be asked how a writer conveys an emotion.
- **Dialogue:** To write out the conversation in script format.
- **Imagery:** The pictures formed in your head from reading the poem, story, etc.
- **Reference:** You can use the text to support your answer. You may be asked to support your answer with reference to the text.
- **Stanza:** The verse of a poem.

Chapter 1
Reading Section

Throughout the English exam, one of the key skills you will be tested on is the ability to read a passage or extract accurately and answer the questions that follow. The first place you will be asked to do this is in the first section of the paper, the reading section.

In this section you will be given a short extract to read and you will be asked to answer the five questions that follow. As this is the first section of the first exam that you will sit in your Junior Certificate, it is designed to be as straightforward as possible. There is no reason why you shouldn't gain full marks on this section as long as you follow a few basic guidelines:

- **Read the extract carefully.** Make sure you understand exactly what the extract is about. If there are any words you don't understand, read the entire sentence again – you may be able to work out the meaning from the context.
- **Read the question carefully!** You cannot gain marks if you don't answer exactly what is being asked. If you are asked to **give reasons** for your answer, then you will need to give at least **two** reasons.
- **Use full sentences in your answer.** At Ordinary Level you are expected to write in full sentences and you may be deducted marks for not doing so.
- **Use the marks given as a guideline.** If a question is only worth 5 marks, then you are only required to write a sentence or two. If it is worth 10 marks, you are required to write a paragraph, and a 20 mark question requires at least two paragraphs.
- **Be neat.** Use the space in your answer book and don't have your answers on top of each other. You should try to create a good first impression. Keep your writing neat and easy to read. Stay between the margins. The answer booklet has margins on both sides of the page.

The margins on the right-hand side are for the examiners, so leave them blank.

- **Be aware of spelling and punctuation.** If there are words that you continually spell incorrectly, then learn how to spell them correctly now.

THE QUESTIONS

Question A is usually broken down into four short questions. Each of these questions usually refers to factual information in the extract and they are worth 5 marks each.

Your answers should be full sentences. Try to put the information in your own words if possible rather than just write out the sentence from the passage.

The other four questions usually relate to your understanding of the text. You will be asked to find certain information in the passage and you may be asked to give your opinion on some aspects of the piece. However, there are certain types of question that are frequently asked, as outlined below.

Find information

In this type of question you will be asked to find out certain facts from the extract and you will usually be told what paragraph of the text to look in. **Only take your answer from the paragraph mentioned.** Also, try to put the information in your own words rather than just copying down the entire paragraph.

Explain the phrases

In this type of question you will usually be given four phrases or sentences, of which you have to explain two. Each explanation is worth 5 marks. In your answers, make sure you use other words rather than reusing the words given. If you are not sure what the phrase means, read the paragraph it comes from, as this may give you a better idea of the meaning of the phrase.

What is the main idea of the extract?

In this type of question you may be asked to pick a topic from a list of three and explain why you think this is the main idea of the passage. Make sure you can give at least two reasons why you think whichever one you choose is correct. Don't be afraid to quote from the extract to support your reasons.

Give your opinion

You may be asked to give your opinion on various different aspects of the passage. For example, you may be asked what type of person you think the writer is. Make sure you give reasons from the passage to support your answer.

The writer

Key words that you could use in your answer:
- **Biased:** If the writer only gives one side of a story or event.
- **Humorous:** If the writer uses funny stories or incidents.
- **Nostalgic:** If the writer looks back on the past.
- **Observant:** If the writer uses a lot of detail in the passage.
- **Optimistic:** If the writer tends to look on the bright side of things.
- **Pessimistic:** If the writer focuses on the bad things.

Style of writing

You may be asked to identify some aspect of the writer's style, such as his use of humour or how he creates a sense of excitement in the piece.
- **Descriptive:** Does the writer use a lot of adjectives or describing words, e.g. 'plastic cups stained with lipstick'? If so, you can say he is very descriptive.
- **Humorous:** Does the writer use a funny incident or describe something in a funny way? If so, you can say he uses humour in his writing style.
- **Repetition:** Does the writer repeat key words or phrases to build up a sense of excitement or suspense in a piece?
- **Short sentences:** Does the writer use short sentences to build excitement or tension, e.g. 'The monster never moved. It just stared at me.'
- **Exaggeration:** Does the writer exaggerate to emphasise or stress his point, e.g. 'The owners of takeaways are responsible for the ruination of society.'
- **Questions:** Does the writer use questions in the piece to address the reader directly or to make you think about the topic?
- **Factual information:** Does the writer use facts and figures to back up his argument?
- **Comparison:** Does the writer compare things to show differences or similarities?

SAMPLE EXAM QUESTIONS

Read the following extract and examine the questions that follow (taken from the 2005 Junior Certificate exam).

'SINK-EATING'

1. Eating as we once knew and enjoyed it has become a thing of the past. A recent survey revealed that the average lunch break in Ireland has slipped to under thirty minutes. But we don't need a survey to tell us that. More meals are eaten in cars than at tables nowadays. A trip around country roads any morning reveals the litter of these moving diners of the night before – plastic cups stained with lipstick, crumpled cartons with the partly chewed remains of instant food, plastic bottles, soiled paper napkins and the menus of some fast food takeaways. The owners of these takeaways are responsible for the ruination of decent society.

2. Nowadays, family meals taken together are unknown. For breakfast, people have pieces of equipment in their cars from which they suck coffee between inhaling exhaust fumes from the lorry they are stuck behind. I recently stood beside a woman in a lift as she ate her breakfast. She began tucking into a sandwich at ground level and had just finished brushing away the crumbs when we reached floor 16.

3. In place of family meals today, we have 'sink-eating' – meals reduced to a moment grabbed between the fridge and the kitchen sink.

4. Despite the fact that we are now living about twice as long as we did a hundred years ago, we seem to be unable to allow enough time to sit down at the table and enjoy the glories of a meal with the rest of the family. It's no coincidence that divorce rates have increased in direct ratio to the decline in family meals. The family that ate together, stayed together. Once we started 'eating on the hoof' – eating while moving around – the family as we knew it was finished. Now, I get sad watching old Hollywood movies and seeing a family all sitting down together and eating in a formal setting. It doesn't happen any more.

Source: Adapted from Peter Cunningham, *Irish Independent*, 7 August 2004

Questions

A.　(i)　What, according to the writer, has become a thing of the past?　(5)

　　(ii)　What has a recent survey revealed?　(5)

　　(iii)　Who or what, according to the writer, is responsible for the ruination of 'decent society'?　(5)

　　(iv)　Name two places where breakfast is eaten nowadays.　(5)

B.　What do we discover about people's eating habits if we drive along any country road? (paragraph 1)　(10)

C.　Explain any **TWO** of the following in your own words:

　　(i)　Moving diners (paragraph 1)

　　(ii)　The lorry *they are stuck behind* (paragraph 2)

　　(iii)　She began *tucking into a sandwich* (paragraph 2)

　　(iv)　'sink-eating' (paragraph 3)　(10)

D.　Is the **MAIN IDEA** of this piece to:

　　advertise fast food?

　　　　OR

　　tell us how families used to eat?

　　　　OR

　　amuse us?

　　　　OR

　　tell us how bad fast food is for us?

　　Give **TWO** reasons for your answer.　(10)

E.　In your opinion, was this article written by a teenager or an older person? Give reasons for your answer.　(10)

Sample answers

A.　(i)　*What, according to the writer, has become a thing of the past?*　*(5)*

　　　According to the writer, eating as we once knew it and enjoyed it has become a thing of the past.

　　(ii)　*What has a recent survey revealed?*　*(5)*

　　　A survey has recently revealed that the average lunch break in Ireland has slipped below thirty minutes.

(iii) *Who or what, according to the writer, is responsible for the ruination of*
'decent society'? (5)
According to the writer, the owners of fast food takeaways are
responsible for the ruination of decent society.

(iv) *Name two places where breakfast is eaten nowadays.* (5)
The writer says that breakfast is eaten in cars and he once saw a
woman eating her breakfast in a lift.

B. *What do we discover about people's eating habits if we drive along any country*
road? (paragraph 1) (10)
If we drive along any country road, we discover that people eat a lot of
food in their cars on the move. The writer says that we would find the
remains of their meals, such as 'the partly chewed remains of instant food,
plastic bottles and soiled paper napkins.'

Use quotations to support your answer.

C. *Explain any **TWO** of the following in your own words:*
(i) *Moving diners (paragraph 1)*
(ii) *The lorry they are stuck behind (paragraph 2)*
(iii) *She began tucking into a sandwich (paragraph 2)*
(iv) *sink-eating' (paragraph 3)* (10)

Make sure you label each answer correctly

(i) 'Moving diners' means that these people eat while they are travelling
in their cars.
(iv) 'Sink-eating' means that people eat while standing between the
fridge and the sink without taking the time to sit down to their meal.

D. *Is the **MAIN IDEA** of this piece to: advertise fast food? **OR** tell us how families*
*used to eat? **OR** amuse us? **OR** tell us how bad fast food is for us? Give **TWO***
reasons for your answer. (10)

> *Any of the choices are correct as long as you can give reasons for your answer.*

The main idea of this piece is to tell us how bad fast food is for us. In the first paragraph, the writer describes the effects on the environment of fast food. He says that 'plastic cups stained with lipstick' and 'crumpled cartons' are found on the sides of the road.

He also tells us that eating this fast food leads to less family meals and thus to higher divorce rates. In fact, he goes so far as to say that the fast food owners are the 'ruination of society'.

E.   *In your opinion, was this article written by a teenager or an older person? Give reasons for your answer.*   *(10)*

I think the article was written by an older person, as he uses phrases like 'eating as we once knew and enjoyed it has become a thing of the past' and the word 'nowadays'. This shows us that he is an older person looking back on the way things used to be. He also seems very nostalgic as he watches old Hollywood movies. This would also suggest that he is an older person.

PRACTICE QUESTIONS

Read the following extracts and attempt the questions that follow.

Before you begin, remember to:
- Read the passage carefully.
- Read the questions and underline the key words.
- Reread the passage and underline the words, phrases or sections that may be useful in your answers.
- Be neat with your answers.
- Use full sentences.
- Only allow yourself 25 minutes to complete the section.

Practice question 1

A MYSTERIOUS LADY (JUNIOR CERTIFICATE 2004)

1. Some time around 1505, Leonardo da Vinci, the great Italian artist, started work on an oil painting of a smiling woman. The picture, which now measures 77 cm by 53 cm, is known as the *Mona Lisa* and it is the most famous painting on planet Earth. All sorts of reasons are given for the *Mona Lisa* being such a popular and well-known painting. Some people say it's because her eyes follow you around the room no matter where you stand, others say it's because her lips appear to quiver as you stare at them, and some art experts claim it's because Leonardo's smoky painting style gives her an air of mystery and excitement. It's said that Leonardo loved this painting so much that he took it with him everywhere he went.

2. He eventually sold it to Louis XII, the King of France, after which the *Mona Lisa* spent her time hanging around posh palaces and magnificent mansions until the time of the French Revolution, when the revolutionaries transferred her to the Louvre art gallery in Paris. When Napoleon came to power, he took her out of the Louvre and hung her in his own bedroom.

3. Since Leonardo painted her, the *Mona Lisa* has been copied thousands and thousands of times. Her face has appeared on tins of Mona Lisa tomatoes, on cocktail napkins, jigsaws and countless other knick-knacks and household objects.

4. No one's quite sure who the woman, Mona Lisa, actually was. Many art experts seem to think she was the wife of a rich merchant called Francesco del Giocondo, which is why she's often referred to as La Giocondo. Other people have even said she could have been Leonardo's mother! The thing that really drives people crazy about the *Mona Lisa* is the mysterious smile that plays around the corners of her mouth.

5. In portraits in those days, people were normally pictured with stern, unsmiling faces (usually their own). So why was the Mona Lisa smirking? Some people have suggested it's because Leonardo employed musicians, comedians and storytellers to entertain her while he was painting her.

Others have said that the picture is actually a self-portrait painted by Leonardo wearing a wig and grinning at his own joke. Someone else has claimed that Mona Lisa's strange smile is the result of other efforts to stop her teeth falling out!

Source: Adapted from 'Leonardo da Vinci' by Michael Cox,
published by Scholastic Ltd

Questions

A. Find answers to the following questions based on the above passage:
    (i)   What is the name of the most famous painting on planet Earth?   (5)
    (ii)   Give one reason why the *Mona Lisa* is such a popular painting.   (5)
    (iii) Who did Leonardo sell the painting to?   (5)
    (iv) Find another name for the *Mona Lisa* in the passage.   (5)

B. Give one example of humour from the text in paragraph.   (5)
    Give a reason why you think it is humorous.   (10)

C. In what way does the *Mona Lisa* differ from other portraits painted in Leonardo's lifetime?   (10)

D. Explain the meaning of the following words as they are used in this passage:
    quiver (paragraph 1)
    posh (paragraph 2)
    knick-knacks (paragraph 3)
    mysterious (paragraph 4)
    smirking (paragraph 5)   (10)

E. Is the MAIN IDEA of this passage:
    to tell us about portrait painting?
        OR
    to inform us about Leonard da Vinci?
        OR
    to show us the funny side of things?
        OR
    to advise us about painting?
    Give ONE reason for your choice.   (10)

Practice question 2

Read the following extract carefully and answer the questions which follow. It is taken in adapted form from *Ireland's Friendly Dolphin* by Sean Mannion.

JUMPING FOR JOY (JUNIOR CERTIFICATE 1996)

1. Fungie is a wild dolphin that came to Dingle Bay, County Kerry, in 1983. He became a great friend of local fishermen and before long tourists were coming from all over the world to see him jump and play.

2. And Fungie is a wonderful jumper. With an almighty surge he leaps from his watery world, shooting through the surface like lightning. He can climb as high as four metres into the air and travel up to a distance of fifteen metres before crashing once more into the sea.

3. He does mid-air twists, loops and back flips. No one can tell which way he will jump next. For Fungie is a wild creature, not a trained performer. It is in the hope of seeing such displays that people crowd Slaidin Strand at the mouth of Dingle harbour.

4. Local fisherman Michael Sheehy, owner of the Silver Fem, has witnessed Fungie's jumping displays. 'We were sailing out one evening and saw three small boats off Slaidin Strand. Fungie went up to the first boat and did five magnificent jumps in a circle alongside. He then swam to the next boat and did five more. He did the exact same number of jumps beside each of the boats.'

5. Fungie also jumps over swimmers, picking the place where he jumps exactly so that he passes close but does not hit them. Kevin McCulloch from Surrey in England experienced just that.

6. Says Kevin: 'A man at the pier said that Fungie was in jumping mood that day. I had no idea how he knew that, but I went out in the boat anyway. I threw a rope out of the boat, slipped slowly into the water and hung on. At first Fungie approached and merely swam by my side. With my goggles on I looked at him looking at me under the water. Then, suddenly, he decided to jump...

7. 'They were extraordinary jumps. He took off on one side, flew high above me and plunged in on the other side. He repeated this again and again for a full five minutes. It is exciting but frightening when a great creature weighing a quarter of a ton is crossing over you. However, he was friendly at all times and I felt confident that he could judge a safe distance from me when coming down. All the same, I must admit that at times it seemed a bit too close for comfort.'

Questions

A. (i)   Where in Dingle do people go to see Fungie jump?   (5)
    (ii) Who told Kevin McCulloch that Fungie was in jumping mood?   (5)

B. Explain the following phrases as they are used in the above extract.
    (i) '…he leaps from his watery world' (Part 2)   (5)
    (ii) '…a bit too close for comfort' (Part 7)   (5)

C. How does the author suggest that Fungie is a big creature?   (10)

D. 'For Fungie is a wild creature, not a trained performer.' (Part 3) From your reading of the extract, do you think Fungie is a wild creature? Give reasons for your answer.   (10)

E. How did Kevin McCulloch feel about Fungie's 'extraordinary jumps'? (Part 7)   (10)

F. Show how 'Jumping for Joy' is a good title for the above extract.   (10)

Chapter 2
Personal Writing

Personal writing means your essay or story. In this section you will be asked to write an essay on one of the given topics. You will be given a wide choice to choose from and it is up to you to decide which topic you will write on. This is your opportunity to gain marks. You don't need any skills other than the ability to write.

As with all the other sections, this one is worth 60 marks. To gain full marks your essay should be at **least** one page (A4) of your answer book but not longer than three pages. It will be difficult during the exam to manage your time well, so don't waste time writing an overly long essay. Regardless of how much you write, the maximum amount of marks available is 60 marks.

THE CHOICES

There is a wide variety of choices in this section.

Story

In this essay you are asked to write a story on a given topic, such as 'The day the plants began to talk'. You may also be asked to write a story that begins or ends with a given line. Or you may be asked to write a story inspired by a photograph or illustration on the paper.

Description

You may be asked to write a description of a given event. The key to this type of essay is to be as descriptive as possible and to stick to the point.

Your thoughts

You may be asked to give your thoughts on a topic. This does **not** have to be a story and you can write about your opinion on the topic.

A dialogue or interview

You may be asked to write a dialogue between two or more people in a certain situation.

A picture

You may be asked to use a given picture as a starting point for a story or discussion.

Diary

You may be asked to write a diary entry for someone on an important day in their life.

Your essay will be rewarded for the following:
- **Content:** The ideas in and the originality of your essay.
- **Expression:** The words you use and how well you use them.
- **Structure:** Your use of paragraphs (beginning, middle, end) and a logical structure in your essay.
- **Mechanics:** Spelling, grammar and punctuation.

THE PLAN

The majority of students look at the exam paper, see a title they think they could write about, pick up their pen and start writing. After the first paragraph (if they have remembered to use paragraphs), they stop writing to decide what they are going to write next, stare into space for 10 minutes and then get worried that they are going to run out of time, so they hurriedly jot down an ending for their story that probably does not make sense (such as a sudden ambush by terrorists) or turn to the old reliable ending, 'He woke up to find it was all a dream!'

If you find that this describes the way your essays usually end up, take a few moments now to consider your options.

- **Option 1:** Keep writing your essays as you have always done and throw away key marks in your exam.
- **Option 2:** Take a few minutes to prepare for this section of the exam.

In addition, keep the following points in mind in relation to your essay.

- **Your essay does not have to be a story:** It is actually very difficult to write a well-structured story in 25 minutes under the pressure and stress of exam conditions.
- **There are other options on the paper:** A dialogue or a diary entry is much easier to write under the time constraints and you don't have to worry about how it is going to end, as those points will be outlined on the paper.
- **You can use an essay you have prepared earlier:** Throughout the school year your teacher will ask you to write essays. See if there is one that was actually quite good and check if you could adapt the titles in the exam to suit your essay.

In the actual exam, your plan could actually be quite brief – just a few notes jotted down reminding you what you want to say in your essay, what should go into each paragraph and how it is going to end.

The most important function of the plan is to stop you from rambling and keep you focused on what you want to say, so make sure you keep checking your plan while you are writing your essay to ensure you are still on track.

STRUCTURE

In addition to having a plan, the structure of your essay is dependent on two things: sentences and paragraphs.

Sentences

Make sure you use capital letters at the beginning of your sentences and full stops at the end. Try to keep your sentences to the point – break up long sentences into two or three shorter ones. It will help make your essay make sense. Don't keep writing phrases like 'And then...and then...' This just makes your essay sound repetitive and boring.

Paragraphs

Use paragraphs in your essay to divide up your story. Every time something new happens, you should start a new paragraph. Each paragraph should begin slightly in from the edge of the page. This will make your essay look much neater and more structured.

Before you begin your essay, you should know what the examiner is looking for in each type of essay.

THE SHORT STORY

If you do decide to write a story, the following are points you should keep in mind. In a short story, the examiner is looking out for plot, characters, setting and using direct speech.

Plot

The story should have a beginning, middle and end. These should make sense and should be **original**. That means that rather than trying to summarise the film you saw last weekend in two pages, you would be better off writing about what you know and making up your own story.

Characters

Good stories have believable characters that are well described to the reader. In other words, don't write a list of names or a list of characteristics, but rather, **describe** your characters.

Don't:
Me and Tim and Carol and Alice and Erica went into town on the bus. Tim was tall and thin, Carol was blonde and tall, Alice was short and had brown hair and Erica was tall as well.

Do:
It was a bright, sunny day so some of my friends and I decided we would go into town on the bus. As usual, Erica and Carol were late and Tim and Alice were going to leave without them. Tim was always a bit short tempered, but Alice kept him calm.

Setting

A story can be set in any time or place you wish, but try to bring the reader into the story by describing the place early in the story. You could describe the houses or clothing of the characters or give descriptions of the locality. Remember to use adjectives or describing words to create a sense of atmosphere.

Read the following extract and examine how the author develops the plot, characters and setting.

FLY, CHEROKEE, FLY (JUNIOR CERTIFICATE 2004)

It started like this: me and Garry Taylor were playing football in the park. I was in goal. I'm always in goal. Garry thinks he's going to be a striker for Arsenal. He likes to prove it by blasting in his 'break the net' shots, which means I have to run miles to fetch the ball. On the night I found Cherokee, the ball had rolled up to the hedgerows near the bowling greens. And there she was, my special pigeon, hiding in the leaf mould under a hedge.

'What are you looking at, Dazza?' Garry shouted, practising his goal scoring celebration wiggle. I waved him to be quiet. He pounded up beside me, as usual. I pointed to the huddled shape among the leaves. He went white with fear and grabbed the ball from me.

'Is it a rat?' he hissed, backing off.

'A rat with feathers?' I tutted at him.

Garry let out a defensive sniff. He turned up his collar just in case.

I crouched down slowly. Cherokee was sitting like a nesting bird, but I couldn't see any sign of eggs. She didn't look well. Her breast was puffed out as if she was cold and her feathers looked dull and broken in places. I pushed my hands forward to pick her up. She made a wooing noise and cocked her head. Her copper eye blinked and she tried to stand. 'I won't hurt you,' I whispered, and closed my hands around her. She stretched a pink foot out, but she didn't struggle.

'If you get bitten and die,' said Garry, 'can I have those trainers with the ticks on the ankles?'

'Quiet,' I shushed him, easing Cherokee out into the open. She blinked again as the light fell on her. Cherokee wasn't like the normal grey pigeons you see. Her wings were a shiny blue-black colour. But her head and breast and tail were white. What you could see of them was white, anyway. 'What you gonna do with it, then?' asked Garry. He was juggling the football and didn't look up. I ran my thumb down the side of her neck. Her feathers felt soft and warm and waxy. I'd never really held a bird before. She weighed about as much as a tennis ball. There was only one thing I could do, really.

'Fly!' I said, and threw her up into the pale blue sky. I knew it was wrong as soon as I'd done it. Cherokee hadn't got the strength to fly. She flapped like mad and nose-dived to earth. Groggily, she picked herself up and settled in the dirt in a miserable ball.

'What am I going to do now?' I said, as Cherokee huddled back under the leaves.

Source: Adapted from *Fly, Cherokee, Fly* by Chris d'Lacey

Questions

1. How does the writer set the scene in the first paragraph?
2. What do we learn about each of the two characters?
3. What words or phrases are used that tell us what kind of people they are?
4. Where does the writer use descriptive words? What effect does it have?

Using direct speech

Direct speech, i.e. what people actually say in quotation marks, is very valuable in an essay. It shows us what type of people the characters are and moves the story along. But the key to using direct speech well is to only use it sparingly and to keep the sentences short.

Look at the extract above. The writer uses direct speech to tell us more about the characters, for example when Garry asks for his trainers if he dies, or to move the story along, such as when the boy shouts 'Fly!' near the end. Try to use direct speech in your essays, but ask yourself two questions first:
- Does it reveal something about the characters?
- Does it move the story along?

If not, don't use it!

STARTING TO WRITE

Your plan

Once you decide on the title you wish to write about, you should jot down your ideas. When you organise your ideas into a sequence, this is your plan. Don't spend any longer than three or four minutes on your plan, as you will not have enough time to write your essay otherwise. You can write your plan either as a list or as a spider diagram.

In a spider diagram, you write the title of your essay in the centre of your page and jot down your ideas around it. You can then number your ideas to decide what order you will write them in and get rid of any ideas you no longer wish to use.

Once you have decided on your sequence, with a beginning, middle and end, you can start writing.

One thing you need to keep in mind is to **keep it simple.** You have 25 minutes to write a story. Stick to describing **one** event with **two** or **three** characters. If you allow your story to be more complicated than that, you will not get it written in the time given.

Fig. 2.1 Sample plan: Spider diagram

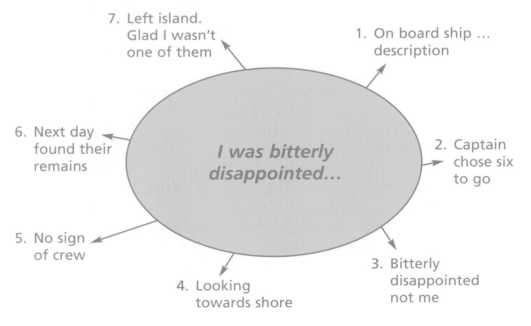

7. Left island. Glad I wasn't one of them

1. On board ship ... description

6. Next day found their remains

I was bitterly disappointed...

2. Captain chose six to go

5. No sign of crew

4. Looking towards shore

3. Bitterly disappointed not me

The opening paragraph

You must try to grab the reader's attention from the opening lines of your story. There are some easy ways to draw the reader in:

- Begin your essay with a **description**. This will bring the reader directly into your story by setting the scene. Use adjectives in your description to help create atmosphere: 'The wind cut through me. My fingers were frozen stiff around my hurl. I was standing in midfield in shorts and thick woollen socks. God, I hated winter training sessions.'
- Begin your story with **direct speech**. This has the advantage of getting straight into the action of your story without wasting time on boring background information: '"Go on, Jack, grab it!" The shouts of the boys below made me forget about the twenty-foot drop to the ground.'
- Use **suspense**. Don't reveal everything in the first sentence. Keep the reader guessing, as this will also keep them interested: 'He walked slowly out of the shop. Maybe they hadn't seen his face. Maybe. He quickened his footsteps until he reached the corner. Then he broke into a run.'

Try to avoid some common mistakes:

- **Don't begin with a list:** 'John and Tony and Sam and Frank went to the circus. They met Ed and George and Sylvia when they got there.' This type of opening sentence is just plain boring.
- **Don't give ridiculous detail:** 'At 8.45 they left for school. At 8.56 they got to school. They went to their first class until 9.40 and then had double PE until 11.00. At break time they each had two chocolate bars and a can of Coke.' This type of information does not add anything to the story, it just makes it dull.
- **Start when your story starts:** 'John and Jason were brothers. They went to the same school and had lots of the same friends. John was ten and Jason was twelve. John liked football but Jason liked basketball. They had a dog and a cat.' Some students tend to write a lot of background information at the beginning of their story. This just stops your story from getting started, especially if none of the information given is important to the story. Get stuck into your story and reveal the important information as it is needed.

The body of your story

Try to make your story as interesting as possible, but also keep it believable. Your story should be between six and eight paragraphs. Try not to race to the end, but rather, describe each step along the way. Use adjectives in your descriptions and try to describe the sounds and smells of a scene, not just the sights.

Conclusion

Your conclusion should be logical. Don't resort to saying 'and then I woke up' at the end of your story. If you have planned it well, you should know how it is going to end. Don't feel that you have to tie up all the loose ends. You are writing your story in 25 minutes, so don't write a very involved story with lots of information filled in at the end.

Practice questions

Keeping the above points in mind, try writing a plan for each of the following essays. Try to write some of them fully and make the opening paragraphs as interesting as possible.

1. The day the plants in the garden began to talk. (2005)

2. 'The first time we met...' Continue the story. (2005)

3. Write a story which at some point includes the sentence: 'I was bitterly disappointed.' (2005)

4. Write a story about an old lady or an old man. (2004)

5. Look at the following illustration. It is a famous painting by the artist Munch, called *The Scream*. Write the story which you imagine gave rise to this painting.

6. '"Don't go outside! Don't go outside! Close all windows and doors..." The message was

repeated over and over again, on all TV and radio stations.' Continue the story. (2003)

7.   'Rise and shine!' Write a story beginning with these words. (2004)

DESCRIPTIVE ESSAY

In this type of essay, you are asked to give a description of an event, person or place. You don't have to write a story for this type of essay, it can just be a description – no characters or plot, just describing something. But you still need a plan! If you don't plan, then you may write a boring, repetitive essay.

Think about your title. Jot down anything that springs to mind. Use the following headings to help you gather your ideas:

- **Sights:** What things do you usually see? People? How are they dressed? Animals? Buildings? Trees? Nature?
- **Sounds:** What do you usually hear? Machinery? Talking? Shouting? Laughing?
- **Smells:** What do you usually smell? Is it pleasant? Unpleasant?
- **Touch:** What can you feel? Cold? Warmth? Pain?
- **Feel:** What is the atmosphere like? Fearful? Excited?
- **Taste:** What does the food taste like?

Use these headings while writing a descriptive essay or short story to add depth to your descriptions.

Sample plan

Describe a trip to a funfair.

- **Sights:** Neon lights, sawdust, Ferris wheel, ticket sellers, stalls, families in groups, crowds of children, shoot the duck, throwing rings, roller coaster, ghost train.
- **Sounds:** Screams of laughter, shouts of sellers: 'Roll up! Roll up!', crying children, clatter of train on track, tinny music, crashes of bumper cars.
- **Smells:** Candy floss, children getting sick, popcorn, oil from machinery, chips.
- **Touch:** Goosebumps of excitement, shiver from gust of wind at the top of the Ferris wheel, butterflies of nervousness in stomach.
- **Feel:** Excitement, nervous, happy, anticipation.

- **Taste:** Salt and vinegar tang of the chips, melt in your mouth sweetness of candy floss.

Read the following extract and take note of how the writer uses description to create a sense of place.

Evening of a hot day started the little wind to moving among the leaves. The shade climbed up the hills toward the top. On the sand banks the rabbits sat as quietly as little, gray, sculptured stones. And then from the direction of the state highway came the sound of footsteps on crisp sycamore leaves. The rabbits hurried noiselessly for cover. A stilted heron laboured up into the air and pounded downriver. For a moment the place was lifeless, and then two men emerged from the path and came into the opening by the green pool.

They had walked in single file down the path, and even in the open one stayed behind the other. Both were dressed in denim trousers and in denim coats with brass buttons. Both wore black, shapeless hats and both carried tight blanket rolls slung over their shoulders. The first man was small and quick, dark of face, with restless eyes and sharp, strong features. Every part of him was defined: small, strong hands, slender arms, a thin and bony nose. Behind him was his opposite, a huge man, shapeless of face, with large, pale eyes, with wide sloping shoulders; and he walked heavily, dragging his feet a little, the way a bear drags his paws. His arms did not swing at his sides but hung loosely.

Source: Adapted from *Of Mice and Men* by John Steinbeck

Questions

1. In the first paragraph, what sounds does the writer mention?
2. What effect does this have?
3. What are the two men wearing?
4. What does this tell us about the men?
5. What physical features of the men are mentioned?
6. What adjectives or describing words does the writer use in his descriptions?

PREPARING YOUR ESSAY

To prepare for this type of essay, think about something you could write a lot about: a club you are involved in? A hobby you have? Your experiences in school? Your family? A typical holiday? An elderly relative?

Jot down all your ideas about this topic. Use the headings on p. 23 to sort out your thoughts. Think about the sights, sounds, smells, etc. associated with your topic.

Using your list, add adjectives to the words. Rather than just saying 'the house was old', you could add **adjectives** and say 'the crumbling old house' instead. Use all your senses to describe the scene: 'The crumbling old house had a faint musty smell.'

Read the following adapted extract taken from the *Life of Pi* by Yann Martel.

In this piece Pi, a sixteen-year-old-boy, has had to jump into a lifeboat as the cargo ship he was on with his family is sinking. The boat was carrying animals from a zoo. Richard Parker is a 450-pound Bengal tiger.

I landed with a trampoline-like bounce on the half-unrolled tarpaulin covering the lifeboat forty feet below. It was a miracle I didn't hurt myself. I lost the life jacket, except for the whistle, which stayed in my hand. The lifeboat had been lowered partway and left to hang. It was leaning from its davits, swinging in the storm, some twenty feet above the water. I looked up. Two of the men were looking down at me, pointing wildly at the lifeboat and shouting. I didn't understand what they wanted me to do. I thought they were going to jump in after me. Instead they turned their heads, looked horrified, and this creature appeared in the air, leaping with the grace of a racehorse. The zebra missed the tarpaulin. It was a male, Grant, weighing over five hundred pounds. It landed with a loud crash on the last bench, smashing it and shaking the whole lifeboat. The animal cried out. I might have expected the braying of an ass or the neighing of a horse. It was nothing of the sort. It could only be called a burst of barking, a kwa-ha-ha, kwa-ha-ha, kwa-ha-ha put out at the highest pitch of distress. The creature's lips were widely parted, standing straight upright and quivering, revealing yellow teeth and dark pink gums. The lifeboat fell through the air and we hit the seething water.

Richard Parker did not jump into the water after me. The oar I intended to use as a club floated. I held on to it as I reached for the life buoy, now vacant of

> its previous occupant. It was terrifying to be in the water. It was black and cold and in a rage. I felt as if I were at the bottom of a crumbling well. Water kept crashing down on me. It stung my eyes. It pulled me down. I could hardly breathe. If there hadn't been the lifebuoy I wouldn't have lasted a minute.
>
> I saw a triangle slicing the water fifteen feet away. It was a shark's fin. An awful tingle, cold and liquid, went up and down my spine. I swam as fast as I could to one end of the lifeboat, the end still covered by the tarpaulin. I pushed myself up on the lifebuoy with my arms. I couldn't see Richard Parker. He wasn't on the tarpaulin or the bench. He was at the bottom of the lifeboat. I pushed myself up again. All I could see, briefly, at the other end, was the zebra's head thrashing about. As I fell back into the water another shark's fin glided right before me.

In the above extract, list what the main character sees, hears and feels.

Not all sentences have to be long. Identify how many short sentences are in the extract. Why do you think the writer does this?

You may also be asked to write a descriptive essay on a person rather than an event or a place. Read the following descriptions of people and identify the techniques the writers use to bring their descriptions to life.

> 'That man is like a cockroach,' Phillis commented. 'Stamp on him and he'll just come out somewhere else.'
>
> The description was apt. He even looked like a cockroach, especially from the back. His shiny cap of greased brown hair emerged from his long rusty coat which was split like a wing case and stuck out over his polished-booted legs. Her description made me laugh out loud.
>
> Source: *Pirates* by Celia Rees, Bloomsbury, 2003.

> For the thousandth time, Meg Finn wondered what she was doing here. How had she sunk this far – skulking around the granny flats with a lowlife like Belch Brennan? Her reflection glared accusingly from the window pane. For a second she saw the ghost of her mother in that face. The same wide blue eyes, the same braided blonde hair, even the same frown wrinkles between

her eyebrows. What would Mam think of this latest escapade? Meg's involuntary blush answered the question for her.

Source: *The Wish List* by Eoin Colfer

Practice questions

Using the following titles, try to write a descriptive essay.

1. Travelling on the school bus. (2005)
2. 'And the winners are...' Describe a competition in which your class or your school or your club has taken part. (2005)
3. The best time of the day. (2005)
4. My dream holiday would be... (2004)
5. My favourite leisure time activity. (2004)
6. Thoughts in a traffic jam. (2003)
7. A day in the country or a day in the city. (2002)
8. The most important people in my life. (2004)
9. Disaster has overtaken the ship in this picture. You are in one of the lifeboats. Write a description of the scene around you.

Exam hints

- Use the extract from the *Life of Pi* on p. 25–6 to give you ideas for this essay.

YOUR THOUGHTS

In the exam you may be asked to give your thoughts on an issue or subject. The titles will usually allow you to write at length about your chosen topic. While these seem to be very straightforward, you need to remember the following:

- You still need to plan your essay. Don't run the risk of writing all you want to say in the first paragraph.
- Your essay still needs to be at least one A4 page.

Sample titles:

- If I were the Taoiseach... (2005)
- Life can't really be enjoyed until you leave school. (2004)
- If I were principal in our school... (2002)
- Teachers – what I think of them. (2000)

The aim in this essay is to be as sincere as possible. You are **not** writing a fictional story, so it would probably be best if you don't plan to start a nuclear war if you were Taoiseach.

Be aware of your audience. You are writing this as part of an exam that will be corrected by teachers, so don't write an entire essay about how dreadful you think teachers are.

You should try to cover different areas in your essay, so think about the different headings you could use in your plan. In an essay where you write about what you would do if you were Taoiseach, for example, you might look at what you would do in areas such as education, health care, local amenities and sport. Your plan might look like the following:

Fig. 2.2 Essay plan 2: If I were Taoiseach

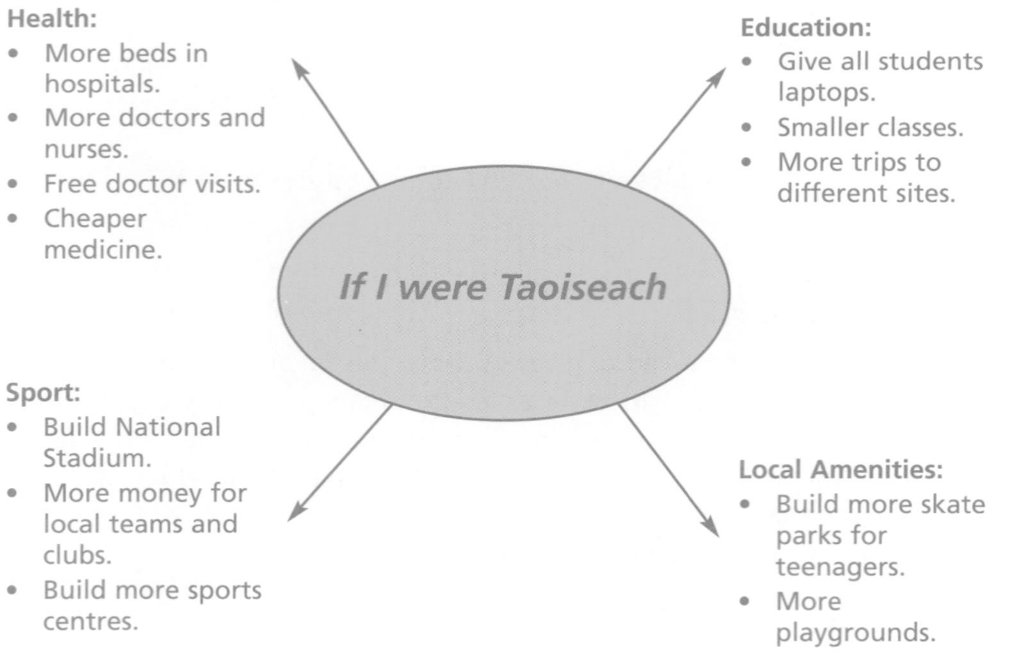

Health:
- More beds in hospitals.
- More doctors and nurses.
- Free doctor visits.
- Cheaper medicine.

Education:
- Give all students laptops.
- Smaller classes.
- More trips to different sites.

If I were Taoiseach

Sport:
- Build National Stadium.
- More money for local teams and clubs.
- Build more sports centres.

Local Amenities:
- Build more skate parks for teenagers.
- More playgrounds.

Read the following passage and identify how the writer puts across his opinion on the subject.

ONLINE SHOPPING

I am never going to buy anything electrical from a high street shop again. From now on it's strictly online shopping for me. This stems from a growing realisation that technology has run well ahead of virtually anybody who works in these shops.

Some time ago, when shopping for components for a home wireless network, I was chatting with a sales assistant about the different pieces of kit when a thought struck me. I asked him, 'You haven't got a clue what I'm talking about, have you?' A little direct, perhaps, but the chap replied quite cheerfully, 'No, I haven't.'

Funnily enough, I think the shops themselves have begun to realise that technology itself is changing the way we shop. A lot of people now do their research online before they make a visit to a store. This is why, for those who do a lot of research, they tend to know more about the products than the people who sell them.

This is having huge consequences, and it's not just about the physical goods: for example, we can access the opinions of thousands of other people about the quality of just about any hotel in the world. This means rip-offs have become less common in a world of free information.

Just how any bog standard retailer is supposed to be able to make money in such a world is beyond me.

Source: Adapted from Chris Johns, *The Irish Times*, 3 May 2006

Questions

1. Why is the writer not going to buy anything from a high street shop any more?
2. What example does he give of his experience?
3. Why do you think he uses this example?
4. What good points does he give about these consequences?
5. Does he give a balanced opinion? How?

DIALOGUE OR INTERVIEW

You may be asked to write your essay in the form of a dialogue or interview. This is a relatively easy option, as the question usually tells you what you need to write about and the structure is very straightforward.

When writing a dialogue, you don't need to worry about using quotation marks or inverted commas. Your dialogue should be written as follows:

Pat: James! How are you doing today?
James: Never better, Pat, never better!

Be aware of the following:
- Your characters' names should be on the left-hand side of the page followed by a colon (:).
- You don't need to use inverted commas (' ').
- You can include background information at the beginning of your piece.
- You can include directions about what the characters should do or how they would say a line. This should be placed in brackets after the character's name.
- You still need to use other punctuation, such as full stops and question marks.
- Keep your dialogue realistic and interesting.
- Allow yourself space to lay out your dialogue clearly.

An interview follows the same format, with the questions and answers each starting on a new line.

Q: So Brad, what are your plans for the future?
A: At present I'm quite busy at home with the kids, but I'm always reading new scripts!

Read the following dialogue and answer the questions that follow.

Teacher: And so, we know then, do we not, that the Boro Indian of the Amazon Basin lives on a diet of...

Perkins: Sir, sir...

Teacher: A diet of...

Perkins: A diet of what, Johnstone? The Boro Indian of the Amazon Basin lives on a diet of what?

Mickey: What?

Teacher: Exactly lad, exactly. What?

Mickey: I don't know.

Teacher (*his patience gone*): Y'don't know. (*Mimicking*) You don't know. I told y' two minutes ago, lad.

Linda: Leave him alone will y'.

Teacher: You stay out of this, Miss. It's got nothing to do with you. It's Johnstone, not you...

Perkins: Sir!

Teacher: Oh, shut up Perkins, y' borin' little turd. But you don't listen do you, Johnstone?

Mickey (*shrugging*): Yeh.

Teacher: Oh, y'do? Right, come out here in front of the class. Now then, what is the staple diet of the Boro Indian of the Amazon Basin?

Mickey (*Looks about for help. There is none.*)

Mickey (*defiantly*): Fish fingers!

Teacher: Just how the hell do you hope to get a job when you never listen to anything?

Mickey: It's borin'.

Teacher: Yes, yes, you might think it's boring but you won't be sayin' that when you can't get a job.

Mickey: Yeh. Yeh an' it'll really help me to get a job if I know what some soddin' pygmies in Africa have for their dinner!

(The class erupts into laughter.)

Teacher *(to class)*: Shut up. Shut up.

Mickey: Or maybe y' were thinkin' I was lookin' for a job in an African restaurant.

Teacher: Out!

Linda: Take no notice Mickey. I love you.

Teacher: Johnstone, get out!

Linda: Oh, leave him alone you. Y' big worm!

Teacher: Right you as well...out...out...

Linda: I'm goin'...I'm goin'.

Teacher: You're both suspended.

Source: *Blood Brothers* by Willy Russell, Menthuen, 2001.

Questions

1. What do we learn about Mickey in this extract? What does he do or say that gives you this impression of him?
2. What type of person is Linda?
3. Write out the dialogue you think would take place in the principal's office.

SAMPLE EXAM QUESTIONS

1. Write out the conversation which might take place between any two rubbish items. (2003)
2. You interview a resident who has lived in Ballybeg since 1950. You ask about the changes during that time. Write out the interview in question and answer form. (2002)
3. You interview one of the survivors of this disaster. (See the ilustration of the sinking ship on p. 27.) Write out the interview in question and answer form. (2001)

PICTURE

On the paper there will usually be a picture to help you find some inspiration for your essay. Make sure you read the question associated with the picture very carefully and that you are clear on what you are asked to do.

You may be asked to:

- Write a short story inspired by the picture. In this case you may use the picture as a starting point and expand on your own ideas from there.
- Write an account of what is happening in the picture. In this case you must stick to the point and use the detail in the picture to guide you.
- Write a conversation between the characters in the picture. In this case use the picture to give you some idea of the characters involved. Try to use detail in the picture to help you.
- Write about the life of a person, animal or object in a picture. You can let your imagination run wild in this essay, but make sure you use the picture to help you.

SAMPLE EXAM QUESTIONS

1. A doll's life. The rag doll in the picture tells her story. (2004)

2. 'My God, Nell! They're like nothing we've ever seen!' Look at the following cartoon and write an account of what you think has surprised the speaker so much. (2005)

3. Write out the conversation between the two animals in the following photo. (2001)

DIARY ENTRY

When you write a diary entry, you should keep in mind what a diary is: a record of your thoughts and reflections on a day's events and your outlook for the future. Therefore, the following guidelines should be adhered to:

- You must write in the first person, 'I', throughout your diary entry.
- Describe the things that have happened to you during the day in the **past tense.**
- Rather than just a list of things that happened, you should include your thoughts and opinions about them.
- You can look toward future events and give your hopes and fears.

Using the illustration of the sinking ship on p. 27 as a guide, attempt the following question from the 2001 exam paper.

What happened on the voyage before the disaster?
Write the story in **diary form**.

Begin like this:

Tuesday, 20 June 2007
A voyage of a lifetime! Cabin – clean and cosy. Great view from porthole…

Chapter 3
Functional Writing

This section of the paper must be answered and is worth 60 marks. You are usually given two choices in this section, of which you have to answer one. The aim of this section is to write **according to the task** required. The language used should therefore be formal, so avoid using slang, abbreviations or text spelling. Make sure you read the question carefully and that you know **exactly** what you are asked to do. The choices in the exam can be broken down into the following categories:

- Informal or personal letter.
- Formal letter.
- Speech.
- Report.
- Instructions, rules and codes.
- Review or blurb.
- Description of a photograph.

As this section is worth the same amount of marks as every other section in your exam, don't think you can get away with writing half a page. Your answer should be at **least** one page of your answer book. Use the space given to make your answer look neat, especially when you are writing a letter. Presentation is important, as it helps you to communicate with the examiner, and it is your skill in communicating that is being tested in this section.

INFORMAL LETTERS

This is the type of letter that you would send to a friend or someone who is known personally to you. The tone and language used should be friendly and it should be obvious that you know this person well.

It is important to be aware of the layout and punctuation, as there are marks awarded for these.

Layout

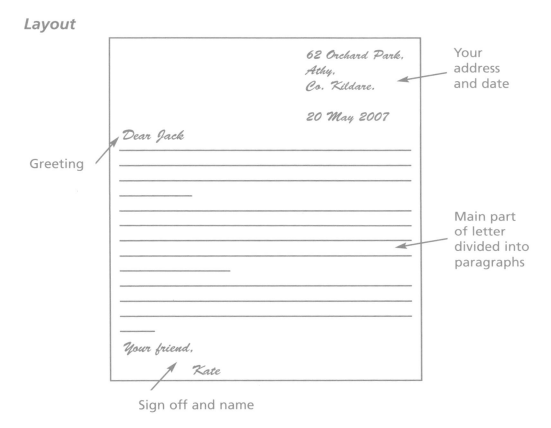

- **Your address:** This should be written at the top right-hand corner of the page. Make sure you leave enough space to fit each line of the address on a separate line. Each line of the address begins with a capital letter and is followed by a comma, except the last one, which has a full stop. (See the example above.)
- **Date:** This can be written in various forms, e.g. 20 May 07, 20-05-07, 20/05/07.
- **Greeting:** In an informal letter, the greeting should be personal and should be just the first name of the person you are writing to.
- **Main part of letter:** Your letter should be personal, so don't forget to ask questions throughout. You need to break down your letter into paragraphs, so each time you start a new topic, you should start a new paragraph.

- **Sign off:** Several versions are acceptable – Your friend, All my love, See you soon, etc. Just make sure that the first letter of the first word is capitalised.

Make sure you answer the question asked. To ensure you stick to the point, a brief plan is useful.

Sample question

Write a letter to a friend you met while on holidays in Spain during the summer. In your letter you should:
- Tell them about your summer since you returned.
- Ask them to visit you in the future.
- Outline some activities you could plan for the visit.

> 25 Ash Drive,
> Newcastlewest,
> Co. Limerick.
>
> 30-07-08

Dear Sarah,

How's life with you? Did you get back OK? Our flight was delayed for two hours on the way back so we had to sit around the airport for ages! Plus it was 2.00 a.m., so none of the shops were open. But we got back eventually, safe and sound.

Did you hear from Pedro since you got back? He did say he would send you an e-mail, but then again, so did Anthony and I haven't heard a thing from him!

What are you doing for the rest of the summer? Would you like to come and visit and stay with us for a week? I know we won't have the same weather we had in Spain, but I'm sure we could find something to keep us amused! There is a big Munster match on next month that I am definitely going to so that could be fun. My dad has also promised to bring me shopping into Limerick so we could do that when you get here.

I hope you can come down soon. Looking forward to hearing from you!

Your friend,
Jessica

Practice questions

1. You are in the Gaeltacht for four weeks. Write a letter home to your parents describing your experiences.

2. Write a letter to your aunt thanking her for the Christmas present she sent you.

3. Write a letter to your best friend who is in hospital. Tell them about things that they have missed in the past week.

4. Write a letter to the *Milan Messenger*, an Italian newspaper, in the hope of finding an Italian pen pal. In your letter, introduce yourself in some detail. Also explain why you are interested in corresponding with an Italian pen pal. (2004)

5. You are Pat, the editor of the advice page of a teenage magazine. Write the reply you would give to one of the following problem letters sent in by your readers. (1997)

   (a) Dear Pat,
   I am fifteen years of age and have just moved to a new school. I have no friends and I am finding it difficult to settle in. I am very unhappy. What should I do, Pat?

   Yours sincerely,
   Miserable

   OR

   (b) Dear Pat,
   I am fifteen years of age and have just done my Junior Certificate examination. A few who were in class with me last year have got jobs and are not going back to school. They have a great time and have plenty of money. I'd love to leave as well. Do you think I should?

   Yours sincerely,
   Confused

FORMAL LETTERS

You may be asked to write a letter in which formal language is used. These letters are written to people you don't know personally. You may be asked to apply for a job or to complain about the service in a restaurant, for example. The structure of a formal letter is slightly different to that of an informal letter. The language used in these letters is very polite and serious. Never use slang or abbreviations.

Layout

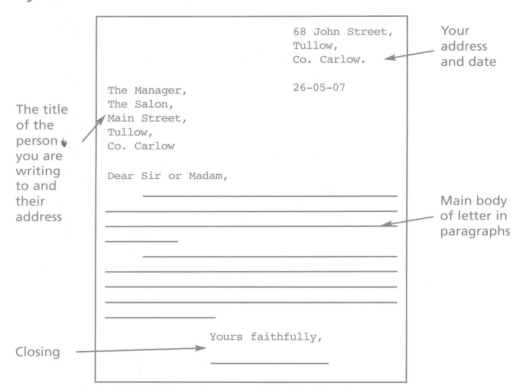

- **Address:** Your address and date should be written as before. The address of the person you are writing to should be written on the left-hand side of the page on the line below the date. You should include the name and title of the person you are writing to if you know it.
- **Greeting:** If you know the name of the person you are writing to, you should address them personally, e.g. Dear Mr Jones. Never use their first name, as this sounds too informal. If you don't know the name, then you should address the letter to 'Dear Sir or Madam' or 'To whom it may concern'.

- **Main body of letter:** Your letter should be divided into paragraphs. Usually two or three paragraphs are enough. Make sure you stick to the point in your letter and answer what is being asked in the question.
- **Closing:** If you have named the person you are writing to, you should end with 'Yours sincerely'. If not, then you should use 'Yours faithfully'.

Sample question

1. Write a letter to a local restaurant where you have received poor service and poor-quality food.

62 The Terrace,
Newbridge,
Co. Kildare.

13-05-08

Mr S. Smith,
The Manager,
The Red Lobster,
Main Street,
Newbridge,
Co. Kildare.

Dear Mr Smith,

    I attended a dinner party in your restaurant on Friday, 10 May. I, along with seven other guests, had made a reservation for 7.30 p.m. to celebrate my brother's birthday. Your staff assured me that this would be no problem.

    From the very beginning of the evening, there seemed to be no end of problems. Our reservation had been overlooked and we had to wait for an hour for another table to become available. Our waitress was rude and failed to deliver any of the correct orders. The dish my brother ordered, the duck, was overcooked and inedible. The cake we had brought was hacked to pieces and the coffee was cold.

    Overall the evening was a very unpleasant experience and ruined my brother's birthday celebration. I expect, at the very least, an apology for the way we were treated and I hope the situation can be rectified to everyone's satisfaction.

Yours sincerely,
Mr Jack Fletcher

Key points

- Stick to the point and answer all parts of the question.
- Use formal, serious language.
- Use paragraphs.
- Use the space given and lay out your answer neatly.

Practice questions

1. You are a resident in a locality affected by the dumping of rubbish. Write a letter to your local county council or corporation. In it you should:
    - Describe the problem.
    - State your annoyance.
    - Make suggestions for dealing with the situation. (2003)

2. Your class decides to raise funds for local charities. You plan to hold a photography competition in your school. Write a letter to the school principal. In your letter you could:
    - Ask for the use of the hall.
    - Explain the purpose of the competition.
    - Describe how you will organise it.
    - Tell how you will advertise it. (2001)

3. Write a letter for publication in your school magazine attempting to persuade students to:
    - Support a charity
      OR
    - Cycle more carefully
      OR
    - Stay healthy. (1996)

4. Answer any one of the classified advertisements below:
    - Eight till late
      Supermarket
      Vacancies for part-time evening work
      Experience useful but not essential
      Applications in writing to Box 54321
    - Beat on the Street
      Music shop
      Wanted

Shop Assistant
Enthusiastic young person with a genuine interest in music
for July and August.
Apply in writing to Box 12345

- Out and About
Sports shop
Part-time work available – Saturdays only.
Teenager would suit.
Applications invited. State interest in sport.
Reply in writing to Box 56789.
(1999)

Exam hints

For a letter of application, there are some key phrases you may like to use.

- I wish to apply for the position of *mechanic*, as advertised in the *Irish Independent* on 12 May.
- At present I am a student in ------ school and I am currently studying for my Junior Certificate exams.
- I have previous experience in this area, as I completed two weeks' work experience in *Murphy's Garage* last year.
- I am hardworking/punctual/dedicated/reliable and eager to learn.
- I am interested in pursuing a career in this area.
- I enclose my Curriculum Vitae and two references.
- I will be available to begin work from 20 June and I look forward to hearing from you soon.

SPEECH

A common question in the Junior Certificate exam is to write a debate speech. In this question you are asked to support one side or another of an argument or motion. The motion will be stated on the paper. The aim of a debate speech is to persuade the audience that your argument is correct. To do this you should support your points using examples, facts and logical argument.

Just as with writing a formal letter, there are a few key phrases that will help you structure your answer.

- **Step 1 – Plan:** Jot down a few ideas for both sides of the argument. See which side of the argument you can write more about and focus on that.
- **Step 2 – Support:** For every point you make, you should be able to support it. Think about examples from books, television, news, etc. that support your side of the argument.
- **Step 3 – Write:** Use the sample introduction on p. 45 to write your first paragraph. Each point you make and the support for that point should be in separate paragraphs. Use the conclusion on p. 46 to help you write your own conclusion.

Overall, your speech should be a minimum of one A4 page.

Sample question

Write a speech for or against the motion that **'all soft drinks machines should be banned in schools'**. You should be either totally **for** or totally **against** this motion. State clearly and convincingly the reasons for your point of view. (2005)

Step 1: Plan

All soft drinks machines should be banned in schools.

For:
- Unhealthy for children.
- Too much sugar, bad for teeth.
- Sugar rush, hyperactive children.
- Lack of concentration.
- Too expensive.

Against:
- Provides necessary liquids after PE.
- Money generated can be used by school to provide equipment.
- Provides service, would just go to the shop anyway.

Step 2: Support

It is probably easier to write an argument *supporting* the motion, i.e. saying that all soft drinks machines **should** be banned in schools.

To support your points, you could outline facts and figures about obesity levels in children. You could look at the situation in America to support your points and you could use your own personal experience.

Remember, this is an English exam, not a court of law, so it is perfectly acceptable to make up your own facts and figures – try to keep them believable, though!

Step 3: Write

- **First paragraph:** This is similar for all debate speeches. Look at the example below and adapt it to suit the speech you are writing.
- **Second paragraph:** You can define the motion. Outline or explain some parts of the motion. For example, in the above motion, you don't want to exclude bottled water vending machines. Focus on the fact that the motion states soft drinks machines. You could also outline your argument.
- **Third, fourth and fifth paragraphs:** Here you make your point, explain your point and support your point. Use facts, statistics or personal examples to support your point.
- **Last paragraph:** You should sum up your points and state again what side of the argument you are on. Look at the sample below for ideas.

Sample speech

Introduction

Chairperson, adjudicators, members of the opposition, friends: we are here today to debate the motion that 'all soft drinks machines should be banned in schools'. My team mates and I totally support this motion.

Points

We, of course, totally support the bottled water vending machines or healthy drinks machines that can be found in some schools. But this motion specifically singles out soft drinks machines, and it is this type of vending machine that my team mates and I are totally against.

It has been proven again and again that these soft drinks are full of sugar and have a severe effect on young children. You only have to look at the effect soft drinks have at a children's party to realise that this can't be good.

Drinking soft drinks during the day can lead to children being hyperactive. This obviously is not a state to be in when you are supposed to be learning. This in turn leads to disruptive behaviour in classrooms and can cause discipline problems for staff and pupils.

You only have to look at the rising levels of obesity in children in the United States to see what will happen here if we continue to allow these machines in our schools. Surely you don't want this to happen?

Lastly, the enormous cost of these drinks machines can place too much pressure on children and parents to have a steady supply of cash to feed into the drinks machine. And who benefits from these machines? Certainly not the children.

Closing

For all of these reasons – the disruptive effect on school life, the negative effects on the health of the children involved and the ridiculous expense of these machines – my team mates and I strongly feel that you should join with us in supporting this motion that 'all soft drinks machines should be banned in schools'.

Thank you.

Hints for speech writing

Remember, you are writing for an audience. Your first paragraph must address the audience you are speaking to. Use the introductory paragraph above as a guideline for writing your opening paragraph. If you are **supporting** the motion, then you are the **proposition** and you will welcome the opposition to the debate. If you are arguing **against** the motion, then you are the **opposition** and you will address the proposition in your opening paragraph.

In the second paragraph, you can define your motion, i.e. highlight the areas you want to focus on and eliminate some of the points that may be used against you. In the example, the second paragraph excluded water vending machines from the argument and focused on the soft drinks machines in the motion. This made the argument easier to make.

You are trying to persuade the audience, so try to win them over to your side by using some of the following techniques:

- Use **obvious questions** (rhetorical questions). Look at the example above. The question, 'Surely you don't want this to happen?' is a rhetorical question. It makes the audience feel they would be right to support your argument.
- Use **examples** that everyone can relate to. In the example, the reference to children's parties is used. Everyone knows what these can be like and so can relate to the point you are trying to make.

In the final paragraph, sum up the points you have made and state again the side of the motion you are on. Finally, thank the audience for listening.

Practice questions

1. Write out your argument for or against the motion that 'Footballers or top models or pop stars are paid too much'. (2003)

2. You have been chosen as a member of the Class Debating Team. The debate motion is 'We should care for our environment'. You need to:
    - Decide whether you are for or against.
    - Think about the points you are going to make.
    - Plan the order in which you will make them.
    - Now write the speech in full. (2002)

3. You have been chosen as a member of the Class Debating Team.
    - Write a list of the points you are going to make on the following topic: It is wrong to keep animals in a zoo.
    - Now, write out the speech in full. (1999)

REPORT

There are two types of report you may be asked to write:

- A news report or article.
- A report on an issue.

News report

A news report for a newspaper is a factual piece of writing. You are trying to tell the reader the key points of the event and give your opinion on why it happened. In a report you could include quotations from eye witnesses and statements from those involved.

The structure of a report is generally as follows:
- Paragraph 1: Who? What? When? Where?
- Paragraph 2: Why?
- Paragraph 3: Quotes or statements.
- Paragraph 4: Outlook for the future.

You may also be asked to write a report on an incident you have witnessed. In this type of report, a similar structure may be followed. The important thing to remember is to include the key information: who? what? when? where? You may also include your opinion of why something happened, but try to keep your report as factual as possible.

Sample question

Write a report for a newspaper on a traffic accident.

CAR CRASH CARNAGE
by John Smith

At approximately 6.15 this morning two cars collided on the main Dublin to Naas road. The two drivers and two other passengers were taken to Naas General Hospital and are said to be in a stable condition.

The icy road conditions may have led one of the drivers to lose control of his car and skid across the central barrier. The temperature last night reached a record low of −8°C and widespread black ice was reported in the area.

A local resident said they heard 'screeching of brakes and a loud bang' at the time reported. A garda spokesman has said that the drivers will be questioned when they are released from hospital. It is uncertain yet if any charges will be brought against the drivers involved.

The stretch of road where the accident took place is known locally as an accident black spot, as four similar accidents have taken place there in the past six months. Residents have asked the Minister to begin a road improvement scheme that has been postponed three times so far. The Minister was unavailable for comment.

Practice questions

1. You have witnessed an attempted bank robbery. Write out the report you would write for the gardaí.
2. Write a report for your local newspaper on an important school match.
3. Write a report for your local paper on an issue that affects your area.

Report on an issue

This type of report is not for a newspaper, but would be given to a group or committee. For example, you may be asked to write a report on proposals for a new school uniform by the principal.

The following headings may be used or changed as necessary:

- **Title:** What exactly is your report about? For example, it could be a report on proposals for a new school uniform.
- **Introduction:** Who asked for the report? Who wrote it? For example, as requested by the principal, carried out by the school council.
- **Research:** What research did you do? Did you carry out surveys? Who did you ask? What type of questions did you ask?
- **Results:** What were the results of the survey? Give percentages. List your findings without giving your opinion.
- **Conclusions:** What conclusions have you reached as a result of this survey? This is where you include your opinion based on the findings you have listed above.
- **Recommendations:** List three or four points that you recommend should happen.
- **Sign and date:** Sign and date the report on behalf of the group.

You don't need to write very much under each of the headings and you can combine some of the sections as it suits you.

Sample question

Write a report on proposals for a new school uniform.

Title: Report on proposals for a new school uniform.

Introduction: As requested by the principal, carried out by the school council.

Research:

We surveyed a wide variety of people to get a well-rounded view of what the new uniform should be. We asked a sample group of students, parents and teachers. The questions we asked looked at all aspects of the uniform and how suitable each new suggestion was.

Results:

- 90 per cent of those asked felt that a polo shirt option should be available for the summer months.
- 40 per cent of those asked felt that the girls should be allowed to wear trousers as an alternative to a skirt, especially in winter.
- 60 per cent of students felt that students should be allowed to wear runners, but 90 per cent of staff and parents said they should wear shoes.
- 20 per cent felt that no uniform should be worn.
- 75 per cent felt that the colours used at present were fine, but that the quality of the jumpers could be better.

Conclusions:

There are many different opinions about the uniform. Regardless of what changes are made, some people will still be unhappy. However, there are some suggestions that the majority of people agree on, and these could be changed immediately.

Recommendations:

- A summer polo shirt should be ordered for the summer months in the school colours.
- More research needs to be done into the option of trousers for the girls.
- The school colours should remain the same, but a new supplier should be found for the jumpers.

Signed:
The School Council
21-05-06

Practice questions

1. Write a report for your local town council about the problem of litter in your area.

2. Write a report for a holiday company on the disastrous holiday you had last summer. Outline the recommendations you would make so that no one else would have to have the same experience.

INSTRUCTIONS, RULES AND CODES

Occasionally in the exam you may be asked to write a set of instructions or rules. The language you use here should be clear and to the point.

- Make sure you understand exactly what is being asked.
- Divide your answer into logical steps.
- Keep your explanations short.
- When writing instructions, detail each logical step and explain any terms used.

Practice questions

1. Your class is making up a town or city code for your area. You have been chosen as class secretary. In *A Code for Our Town,* the class points out:
    - What should be done.
    - What should not be done.
    - Why.

    Now, write *A Code for Our Town* in full. (2002)

2. Write out the rules of a photography competition. In the rules you should mention:
    - The different groupings of pictures.
    - The different age groups involved.
    - The regulations about entries.
    - The prizes to be won. (2001)

3. Descriptions of games for teenagers are to be included in a millennium time capsule. You wish to contribute a description of a game you like. For future teenagers:
    - Describe how the game is played.
    - List some of the main rules. (2000)

REVIEW OR BLURB

A **review** is your opinion of a book, film, CD, etc. When you are writing a review, you should include the following:

- The full title of the film, book or CD along with the name of the director, author, band, etc.
- Possibly some background information.
- A summary of the book, film or CD, but don't give away the important parts, such as the ending of the film.
- Your opinion. Highlight the high points and discuss the weaknesses, but try to be balanced.
- If you liked it, you should be enthusiastic and encourage others to see it/hear it.

A **blurb** is the written text on the back of a book or DVD cover. It usually contains an outline of the plot, gives details of the characters and the actors playing them and tries to promote the book or DVD. The main function of a blurb is to get you to want to buy the book or DVD, so it is always full of praise with no negative comments.

Sample review

> MISSION IMPOSSIBLE III
> Directed by J.J. Abrams
> Starring: Tom Cruise, Philip Seymour Hoffman, Ving Rhames, Michelle Monaghan
> 12A Cert
>
> Starting the summer blockbuster season with a big bang, *Mission Impossible III* raises the bar for all the mega-budget action extravaganzas to follow in the weeks ahead. J.J. Abrams, making a start as a director after his experience on *Lost* and *Alias*, was an inspired choice to helm this adrenalin-pumping adventure.
>
> Abrams ignores the Bond-like opening sequence that has seemed normal for the genre and immediately gets down to the business of heroes and villains as Owen Davian (Philip Seymour Hoffman) gives secret agent Ethan Hunt

(Tom Cruise) a countdown to 10, during which he has to reveal the location of a rabbit's foot or a tied up woman will die.

Hoffman makes Davian a formidable enemy, an unscrupulous, conscience-free black market trader in weapons and information, regardless of the human consequences.

The set pieces are spectacular, as they need to be, and orchestrated with remarkable cinematic flair and exemplary stunt work. Crucially, the movie gets its priorities right, in that its many special effects are there to serve the story, rather than the other way round. Abrams propels the action at such an accelerated pace that there's barely time to draw breath.

Source: Michael Dwyer, *The Irish Times*, 5 May 2006 (adapted)

Practice questions

1. Write a review of any TV drama series you watch regularly. In the review you might refer to:
    *   The setting.
    *   The main character.
    *   The quality of the acting. (1997)

2. Write a review of a film you have seen recently. In your review, you should include:
    *   Name of the film.
    *   A brief summary of the plot.
    *   In your opinion, the high point of the film (actors? setting? special effects?).

3. Write the blurb for the back of the DVD cover of a film you enjoyed.

DESCRIPTION OF A PHOTOGRAPH

If you are asked to write a detailed description of a photograph, you should keep the following points in mind:
*   State the obvious. Say if the photograph is black and white or colour, if it is a landscape or a portrait of people, etc.

- Divide the photograph into sections and describe each one separately: 'In the background there is…', 'In the middle ground we see…', 'In the foreground there is…'.
- Describe the expressions on the faces of the people involved: 'He is smiling and looks relaxed and happy.'
- Describe the atmosphere: 'It looks dark and bleak because…', 'It looks happy and cheerful because…'.

Practice questions

1. Write accurate descriptions of the following photographs.

(a)

(b)

(c)

(d)

Chapter 4
Media Studies

The Media Studies section may appear in section 4, 5, 6 or 7 of the paper. If it appears in section 4, then it is a **compulsory** question. In this section you are expected to be able to answer questions on different types of media, such as advertising, newspapers, information leaflets, signs and television.

As with all the other sections on this paper, this section is worth 60 marks and you should spend approximately 25 minutes answering the questions. Make sure you look carefully at the marks awarded for each question. A question worth 20 marks will obviously require more work than a 10 mark question.

You will be given a sample from the chosen media on the exam paper and you will be asked to examine it carefully and answer the questions that follow. As this usually involves a visual aspect, there are some **key points** common to all the media that you should be familiar with and be able to use in your answer.

PURPOSE

The first thing you need to decide is the **purpose** of the piece. What does it want to do? Advertising wants to persuade us to buy the product, a newspaper article wants to inform us of an event and an information leaflet wants to educate us in a certain area. Once you have identified the purpose, it is easier to see the techniques used to achieve this aim or purpose.

You should also be able to identify the **target market** for this piece. Who is it aimed at? Sometimes the target market is pictured in the visuals, but be careful – an advertisement for hair shampoo may be aimed at the type of people pictured in the visuals, but the target market for nappies isn't babies (as they can't buy them), but the parents, as they do the shopping.

VISUALS

When you examine the Media Studies sample included on the exam paper, you will see two things:

- The written words.
- Everything else.

'Everything else' is the visual element. This includes the colours used in the background, the people depicted, the font, size and shape of the letters. All of these things are used for a reason. Your job in the exam is to try to identify and explain why they are used.

COLOURS

It is useful to know why certain colours are used. Some colours are associated with ideas or feelings. Red, for example, is associated with love and passion but also with danger. Green is associated with nature and freshness, which is why it is often used in advertising for cleaning products. Look at the colours used. Why do you think they are used? What could they be associated with?

PEOPLE

People in an advertisement or information leaflet can tell you a lot about who it is aimed at. Look at the clothes worn, the situation they are in and especially their facial expressions. All of these things will reveal key elements of the advertisement, leaflet, etc. Do the people have cheerful expressions? Is the product associated with their happiness? Do these people represent the target market? Are they used just to grab your attention? Is a celebrity used?

ENDORSEMENT

Sometimes a celebrity is used in an advertisement to promote it. This is called celebrity endorsement. Many sports brands use sports stars to promote their products. Sometimes a famous person may allow their name to be associated with a cause they believe in, such as Bono and the 'Make Poverty History' campaign.

BACKGROUND

Look at the background in the sample given on the exam paper. Remember, it was chosen for a reason. Why do you think this background was chosen? Is it very plain, making the key points stand out? Is it very dark, giving a very grim or bleak appearance? Or is it bright and cheerful, giving a positive view? Is there any feature that stands out or is unusual? Why do you think it was used?

LETTERS

Look at the letters used in the writing on the sample on the exam paper – not what they say, but how they are presented. Are they large and do they dominate the space? Or are they small and insignificant? What colour is the writing? Look again at the meaning of certain colours. Is red used to grab your attention or simply black and white? Why do you think certain colours are used? Look at the type of writing or the font that is used. Does the writer use a very old style or a modern, sleek style? Why do you think this style was chosen?

LOGO

A logo is a symbol associated with a product or service. Some logos are very recognisable, such as the Nike logo, while you may not have seen others before. A logo is used to sum up the company and represents what they are about. Check if there are any logos in the sample on the paper. What do these logos tell you about the company involved? What colours are used? Do they stand out? Why?

TEXT

In any advertisement, information leaflet, set of signs or photographs, there will usually be some writing. This is the text. You have already looked at how it is written, but now you need to look at what exactly is said. You need to identify if any of the following techniques are used.

Slogan

A slogan is a phrase associated with a product or service. The Nike slogan is 'Just do it!' Some are short and catchy and get straight to the point. To make them sound catchy, sometimes rhyme is used: 'A Mars a day helps you work, rest and play' or alliteration (using words that begin with the same letter): 'If you want to have a cuppa have a Club'.

Facts

Some advertisements or information leaflets use a lot of factual information to try to persuade you that they are correct. It is up to you to identify the statements that are factual and those that are only opinion. Look out for language that sounds scientific or the use of statistics, e.g. '90 per cent of cat owners said their cats preferred it'.

In advertising in particular you may find some of the following features:

- **Buzz words:** Words that are used to make the product sound more attractive. There are usually words associated with certain areas, e.g. skin care uses buzz words like 'age-defying' and cars use words like 'aerodynamic'.
- **Rhetorical questions:** Questions that do not require an answer, e.g. 'Are you tired of the same old boring holidays?'
- **Punctuation:** Sometimes punctuation is used to give the written text some excitement, such as using exclamation marks!!
- **Special offers:** Some advertisements include special offers or discounts to try to persuade you to buy the product and to grab your attention.
- **Orders:** Some advertisements give you orders, telling you to do something, e.g. 'Buy this product', 'Just do it!'

Exam hints

Most examples of Media Studies use either:

- Visuals only.
- Text only.
- A combination of text **and** visuals.

The most effective of these is the combination of both text and visuals.

In your answers you should try to include as many of the key words above as possible to explain why it is effective or why you like it.

Practice questions

Examine the following examples and identify the key points of each.

ADVERTISING

1. Describe the logo in this advertisement. Why do you think these colours were used?
2. What is the slogan?
3. What are the key words associated with this product?
4. What is the main point about this product that is made in this advertisement?

1. What is eye catching about this advertisement?
2. What are the key colours?
3. How do they relate to the product?
4. Who do you think this product is aimed at?

5-A-DAY THE HEINZ WAY.

Heinz Baked Beans in Tomato Sauce, made with select beans and ripe tomatoes, contributes towards your recommended five daily portions of fruit and vegetables as part of a healthy, balanced diet. www.heinz.co.uk

1. What is striking about the visual used?
2. What are the main colours used? Why do you think they are used?
3. What words or phrases are used in the text to persuade you to buy the product?

INFORMATION LEAFLETS OR BROCHURES

Information leaflets or brochures try to give you information, but also try to persuade you to carry out a certain action. The techniques used in advertising can also be found in brochures and information leaflets.

Examine the following and answer the questions that follow.

Practice questions

1. What do you think is meant by the phrase 'Be part of the bigger picture'?
2. What is striking about the visuals on the front of the leaflet?
3. Why is Census 2006 so important?
4. What type of questions are on the census form?

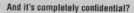

What is the census?

The census, which takes place every five years, is a count of all the people and households in the country.

The next census will be on Sunday April 23rd, 2006, when everyone who is in the country on that date will need to be included on a census form.

No matter where you are on census day - whether you're at home, staying with relatives or friends, in a hospital, etc – you will need to be counted.

And only by every one of us being counted will the census work for all of us.

You see the census is a bit like a jigsaw really. Unless we have all the pieces we simply won't be able to get the complete picture.

Why is Census 2006 so important?

The census is more important than ever because the picture has changed so much over the last few years.

We are living in a rapidly changing Ireland; in a diverse and vibrant Ireland, and the census is the only way we can accurately track the significant demographic and social changes that are taking place in our society.

The answers you give on your census form provide the vital information we need to plan a better future for all of us.

Only by all of us being part of the bigger picture, can we accurately plan future economic and social policies and services in areas such as housing, health, education and childcare.

How does it involve me?

Remember, the census can only truly work if absolutely everyone is included. That's why every household in the country will receive a census form. Then, on census day - Sunday April 23rd, 2006 - the householder or any adult member of the household present that night must fill it in.

Is it compulsory for me to fill in a census form?

Yes. Because the information the census provides is so important for planning a better future for us all you are obliged by law to fill in a census form.

What kind of questions are on the census form?

There are two types of questions on the census form: those relating to accommodation occupied by the household and then questions relating to individuals who reside there on census night.

Remember, it is only by answering every question accurately that we can ensure that we'll all be part of the bigger picture.

And it's completely confidential?

Absolutely. All of the answers you provide on your census form are completely confidential. This is guaranteed by law!

The Central Statistics Office, which carries out the census, can only use the data for statistical purposes. It is forbidden by law to disclose any information on individuals or households to any person or organisation, including any other Government Department or Agency.

So what happens next?

Every community in Ireland, including yours, has a number of Census Enumerators – people employed by the Central Statistics Office to carry out the census.

Your Census Enumerator will make contact with you to deliver your blank census form. Please keep your form safe and complete it accurately on census night. Your Census Enumerator will then call to collect your completed form as soon as possible after census day.

Remember, the census can only truly work if everyone takes part.

CARTOONS

There are two types of cartoons found in the media: political cartoons and humorous cartoons.

Political cartoons, such as the example below, are there to make fun of a current political situation or to point out serious issues in a humorous way.

The other type of cartoon is not political but is just trying to be funny. These cartoons, such as Denis the Menace or Garfield cartoons, are often found at the back of newspapers and may continue on from day to day.

You may be asked questions about the characters in these cartoons and what they are doing. There are some things you need to bear in mind:

- Only refer to the cartoon on the paper. It doesn't matter if you know that Denis the Menace always annoys his next-door neighbour – if it isn't on the paper, you can't refer to it in your answer.
- Use all the information on the paper to help you. Look at what the characters **do** and what they **say**. They will be the key points in your answer.

Practice Questions

1. What is the main point being made by this cartoon?
2. What problems does the artist outline?
3. What type of newspaper do you think this cartoon would appear in?

1. What do you learn about Denis in this cartoon?
2. What do you think makes this funny?
3. What other characters do you learn about?

PHOTOGRAPHS

In the exam, you may be asked to examine a photograph or series of photographs in this section of the paper.

- Examine the photographs and make sure you understand exactly what is being depicted or shown.
- Look at the questions asked. If you are asked to describe a photograph, look back at the hints for describing photographs on pp. 53–4.
- You may be asked to group the photographs or to give a title or written text for the photographs. See if there are any logical links between the photos. Do they contain children or animals? Do they show a particular activity? Do they capture a certain time of day? Is there anything interesting about the way the photograph has been captured?

There are some technical terms that may help you to examine the photographs.

- **Foreground**: The area at the front of the photo.
- **Background:** The area at the back of the photo.
- **Focus:** The area or item in the photo that grabs your attention. It is usually found at the centre of the photo and the image is sharp, not blurred.
- **Low angle shot:** Where the camera is below the object being photographed and looking up. This type of shot makes things appear larger than they are and therefore more threatening.
- **High angle shot:** Where the camera is above the object being photographed and looking down. This type of shot makes things appear smaller than they are and thus less threatening.

Practice questions

Examine the selection of photographs and answer the questions that follow.

1. For a photography exhibition you must arrange the photographs into two or three groupings. Give a suitable name to each grouping.
2. Choose one photograph you feel stands out. Describe the photograph accurately. Explain why you think it stands out.
3. Write a caption and a brief written introduction that could be included with the photograph in question 2 at the exhibition.
4. Which photograph do you feel is the least interesting? Give reasons for your answer.

Practice questions

Look carefully at the following and answer the questions that follow.

Don't swim alone

Learn to use equipment before trying it out

Remember These Rules: Enjoy Yourself: Come Home Safely!

Captions

1. Do not overload the boat – this will make it unstable
2. Do not swim just after eating
3. Check locally concerning dangerous currents, strong tides, etc.
4. Do what the lifeguard tells you
5. Do not drink alcohol while setting out or during your trip
6. Do not swim out to sea

1. Look carefully at pages 68 and 69. Now, match the cartoons lettered A–F with the captions numbered 1–6. One match has been made for you as an example – example: B–6. Now write the remaining five matches in your answer book. (10)
2. Which of the cartoons A–F do you find the funniest? Give reasons for your answer. (10)
3. Look carefully at cartoon G on this page. Now, write a suitable caption for this cartoon. (10)
4. Refer to cartoons 1 and 2 on page 67. Which cartoon do you think is better? Give reasons for you answer. (10)
5. Look at picture 3 on page 67. It shows dangerous conditions at sea. Write a headline and a description of the weather for the front page of your local newspaper. (20)

Exam hints

In the past few years, the last question in the Media Studies section has asked you to carry out a written task. Look back at Chapter 3 for details on how to write reports, reviews, etc.

NEWSPAPERS

There are two different types of newspaper that you need to be aware of: tabloid and broadsheet. You need to be able to identify the key features of each.

Tabloids:

- Smaller size.
- Large headlines, exaggerated.
- Many photographs.
- Block headlines.
- 'True life' stories.
- Celebrity gossip.
- Paparazzi photos.

Broadsheets:

- Larger size.
- Factual headlines.
- Fewer photos, more written text.
- Longer articles.
- Politics/world affairs/business.
- Analysis of events.
- Photos from abroad.

The main difference between these two types of newspaper can be seen in the layout of the front page. In a tabloid newspaper, the front page is usually dominated by one story with a large photograph, a block headline and very little written text. In a broadsheet newspaper, the front page usually contains a number of stories with a smaller photograph and a lot of written text.

Look at the examples of newspapers that follow and answer the questions.

Practice questions

Daily IRISH Mail

TUESDAY, JUNE 13, 2006   www.dailymail.ie   V1   50c

THIS PAPER COSTS JUST 50c

HIAWATHA

FREE CHILDREN'S CLASSIC DVD

PICK UP FROM EASON OR DUNNES (GROCERY) STORES OR WE CAN POST THE WHOLE COLLECTION TO YOUR HOME   DETAILS: PAGE 30 P&P PAYABLE

HAUGHEY: A FINAL VIGIL

Family gather at his bedside as medics say he has only days left

FORMER taoiseach Charles Haughey has just days left to live.

The 80-year-old disgraced politician, who was first diagnosed with prostate cancer in 1995, has suffered a serious deterioration in his condition.

Last night, his family maintained a bedside vigil at his beloved Abbeville home, where they have been gathering throughout the weekend.

Sources say that Mr Haughey's personal physician told his family that he was unlikely to live more than three or four days.

It is believed that the former Fianna Fáil leader has been drifting in and out of consciousness, and that doctors are concentrating their efforts on mak-

By Ronald Quinlan
Political Correspondent

ing him as comfortable as possible in his last hours.

Last night, a close friend of the Haughey family said that while they had been fearing the worst since the former taoiseach was discharged from the Mater Private Hospital on April 7, his deterioration on Friday night had taken them by surprise. But they are said to be resigned to the inevitable.

'They are doing quite well under the circumstances. It is a very sad time, but it has been coming for a long time and everybody is now doing what they have to do,' said the friend.

Insiders say that arrangements for a State funeral are already in place and that representatives of **Turn to Page Six**

The end of an era for football as Roy Keane hangs up his boots

SEE PAGES 8, 9, 10 & 11 AND BACK PAGE

1. What is the main headline?
2. What are the dominant colours used?
3. What do you think is the most eye-catching part of this front page?
4. Would you buy this paper? Why or why not?

Irish Independent

IRELAND'S BEST-SELLING DAILY NEWSPAPER

FAREWELL KEANO

JAMES LAWTON, RONNIE WHELAN, GERRY McDERMOTT,
AND DERMOT BOLGER PAY TRIBUTE NEWS & SPORT

WWW.INDEPENDENT.IE TUESDAY 13 JUNE 2006 €1.60 (75p IN N. IRELAND)

Family's vigil as Haughey health worsens

Arrangements for a full State funeral are already in place

Gene McKenna, Fionnan Sheahan and Sam Smyth

FORMER Taoiseach Charles Haughey is near death after his health took a serious turn for the worse.

Close family members kept a bedside vigil at Mr Haughey's Abbeville mansion in Kinsealy last night after his condition deteriorated rapidly in recent days.

Sources close to the family said they were just trying to make the ailing former Taoiseach as comfortable as possible during his final days.

Family and friends are now said to be resigned to the fact that Mr Haughey is unlikely to survive his latest illness.

"There is a feeling that it is now just a matter of time and doctors have done all they can," a family friend said.

"Things are not good. The situation got much more serious over the weekend. The next few days will be vital. This is the worst he has been since he first became ill."

The *Irish Independent* has also learned that arrangements have been made for a State funeral for the former Taoiseach.

Mr Haughey approved the arrangements last year.

It is understood he asked for a Requiem Mass to be held in Our Lady of Consolation Church in Donnycarney, in the heart of the Dublin North Central constituency he served rather *Continued on Page 7*

Roy This time, it really is goodbye . . .

THE long goodbye culminated with a final farewell from Roy Keane yesterday, his body having reached breaking point after a glorious career of superhuman endeavour.

The end, when it came, was uncharacteristically understated, a brief statement on Celtic's official website confirming that medical advice had forced him to succumb to a hip injury and thus to the inevitable reality he has spent so long trying to postpone.

Keane, pictured last month with one of his children, had been talking about retirement for so long, almost from the moment he left the Ireland camp on the eve of the 2002 World Cup finals.

He retired from international football immediately, only to return before departing again.

There followed an acrimonious departure from Manchester United last autumn, paving the way for a brief swansong with Celtic, the fulfilment of a lifetime's ambition.

KEANE BOWS OUT: PAGES 8,9,12,22 & 23

Four die in 15 hours on roads

ROAD carnage saw four more lives lost in a series of accidents over a 15-hour period. The relentless spiral of deaths has seen the toll rise to 182 since the beginning of the year.

Two of the fatalities were motorcyclists, who, according to statistics, are six times as likely to be killed on our roads than drivers.

Yesterday morning, 21-year-old Stephen Curry was killed after his car struck a wall at Kilbreaet, Co Clare. An elderly woman was killed in a car crash in Newport Co. Mayo.

FULL STORY, PAGE 4

Medical graduate found strangled in city apartment

Brian McDonald

A YOUNG female doctor who was due to graduate from college next week has been found strangled in a city centre apartment.

A man was being questioned by gardai last night following the discovery of the body of Karen Guinee (24) in Galway yesterday morning.

The victim, who is originally from Cork, had just completed her medical studies in recent weeks.

Her parents were due to travel to Galway for her university graduation cere-

many next week. Instead, the devastated couple had to undergo the heartbreaking task of identifying their daughter's remains.

Karen is believed to have been strangled.

Gardai found her body at the apartment over Hogan's chemist shop in Fr Griffin Avenue, just a 10-minute walk from Galway city centre, at about 6.30am.

A 27-year-old man was also at the apartment.

He apparently also suffered minor injuries and was taken by ambulance to nearby University College Hospital Galway where he received medical treatment.

Following his discharge

from hospital, he was arrested by gardai and taken to Mill St station.

The man was detained for questioning under Section 4 of the Criminal Justice Act.

His initial six-hour period of detention was extended by a further six hours yesterday afternoon.

The young woman had sat her final medical exams at NUI Galway only recently and was preparing for her graduation ceremony scheduled at the Galway university for next week.

Originally from Donegal in Cork, she had been living in Galway while completing her studies.

Continued on Page 4

Al-Qa'ida chooses new leader

AL-QATDA in Iraq yesterday named its new leader and vowed to keep up a campaign of beheadings and suicide bombings.

The warning came on a day when violence, including two car bombs, killed at least 34 people.

Sheikh Abu Hamza al-Muhajir was chosen to succeed Abu Musab al-Zarqawi, who was killed last week.

An al-Qa'ida statement said the new leader "had a history in jihad and is knowledgeable. We ask God that he continue what Sheikh Abu Musab began".

FULL STORY, PAGE 36

NEWS

Hope fades for ill GAA star

The family of GAA star Jason Gilligan (38) who suffered a brain haemorrhage were keeping a vigil at his bedside last night. **Page 6**

Abuser's jail term too lenient: minister

The British Home Secretary has called on the courts to reconsider a five-year sentence for a paedophile who abused a three-year-old girl. **Back Page**

SPORT

How All Black sharpens edge

Faith and hard work are the forces that have given All Black powerhouse Rodney Sofuala his edge. **Page 26**

Kernan: Give counties more cash

Armagh boss wants gate receipts from replayed championship games distributed more fairly among the counties. **Page 25**

Features P14
The world according to Ian O'Doherty

BUSINESS

Waterford group back in profit

Restructuring at Waterford Wedgwood should allow the crystal and china group to record an operating profit in the current financial year. **Page 19.**

ECB warns of more interest rate hikes

Less than a week after interest rates rose ECB policymakers are warning that more rises are on the way. **Page 18.**

Inside: Kevin Myers salutes the veterans of D-Day **Page 12**

---

1. How many different stories are featured on this page?
2. What are the dominant colours used?
3. Would you buy this newspaper? Why or why not?
4. What are the main differences between this paper and the tabloid newspaper?

MAGAZINES

Magazines are aimed at different readers. You can identify who they are aimed at by looking at the type of stories included, the photos used and the products that are advertised. For example, a magazine about football is not going to contain an advertisement for make-up.

Look at the following contents page for a magazine and answer the questions that follow.

Practice questions

1. What type of stories are in this magazine?
2. What colours are used to grab your attention?
3. Who do you think this magazine is aimed at?
4. List four products that you think would be advertised in this magazine.

TELEVISION AND RADIO

Look at the following schedule and answer the questions that follow.

Monday September 25

RTÉ One

Watch it! The Afternoon Show, 3.00pm, RTÉ One

RTÉ Two

Watch it! Legend, 9.30pm, RTÉ Two

TG4

Watch it! Hector San Oz, 10.30pm, TG4

TV3

Watch it! Malcolm in the Middle, 8.00pm, TV3

RTÉ One

6.00 Act of Will 62819038 6.55 Euro News 45494632 8.00 Neighbours (R,S) 81126019 8.25 Dallas 53771125 9.20 The Afternoon Show 3771125 9.20 The Afternoon Show (RTÉ News, Weather) 14982038 10.40 Dr Phil "Trapped" (RTÉ News, Weather) 13626458 11.30 Shortland Street 46332477 12.00 Reba Sitcom. 48532941 12.30 Fair City (S) 96954146 1.00 RTÉ News: One O'Clock (Weather, Cinnlinte Nuachta) 18748274 1.25 Home and Away Lucas is interrogated at the police station. Cassie is delighted when Macca returns – but she doesn't know that he has started taking speed. (S) 18756293 1.55 5 Star Series following the opening of a five-star hotel. (R) 69095564 2.25 EastEnders (R,S) (RTÉ News, Weather) 51675903 3.00 The Afternoon Show Daytime entertainment show presented by Blathnaid Ni Chofaigh and Sheana Keane with a mix of lifestyle, showbiz news, fashion and cookery. (RTÉ News) 42954564 4.25 Hope and Faith Sitcom that brings together two very different sisters. With Faith Ford. 54712380 4.50 Doctors "Mountains to Climb" 28898629

5.20 Nuacht RTÉ (Followed by News for the Deaf) 45668598
5.30 The Bill "Compulsion"(Part 1) (S) (European Weather and The Angelus) 87723632
6.01 RTÉ News: Six One (Followed by Weather) (S) 95586075
7.00 Nationwide (S) 37842125
7.30 Scannal (New Series) Scannal looks back at the amazing story surrounding the death of Fr Niall Molloy. 65330564
8.00 EastEnders Owen has vanished after threatening to kill himself. 37828545
8.30 Househunters in the Sun With Jim Smyth. 37830380
9.00 RTÉ News: Nine O'Clock (Followed by Weather) (S) 46304212
9.30 Junior Doctors The four interns must decide which career in medicine to pursue. (Last in series) 24321941
10.20 Questions and Answers With John Bowman. 38776941
11.20 City Folk Documentary magazine examining the lives of people in European cities. 38152090
11.55 RTÉ News and Weather (Followed by an Evening Prayer) 13803090

12.00 The Late Late Show Second chance to see last Friday's show. (R,S) 53799826 2.00 Questions and Answers John Bowman chairs the discussion. (R,S) 40949268 2.55 Water Rats – Double Bill Drama series set in and around Sydney Harbour. 83388268 4.25 Shortland Street (R) 26947152 4.50 Nationwide Reports from around Ireland, presented by Michael Ryan and Mary Kennedy. 11179978 5.15 Dr Phil (R) 24464355

RTÉ Two

6.00 Farthing Wood 30245380 6.25 Morbegs 27714944 6.40 Horrible Histories 85491090 7.35 Wakey Wakey: DDN (R) 62494361 8.00 Bravestarr 81117361 8.25 Cyborg 009 89011564 8.50 Roobarb 12746212 9.00 Den Tots: Balamory 65646106 9.25 Bear in Blue House 65649293 9.55 Storylane 23045835 10.00 Barney 23658670 10.30 PICME 74062545 10.40 Tweenies 32014670 11.05 Save-Ums! 95916380 11.15 Cooking for Kids 75983767 11.20 Morbegs 41857090 11.40 Blanche 89132748 11.45 Noddy 41632632 11.55 Thomas 41638816 12.05 Fimbles 50415421 12.30 Fifi 10556670 12.40 Balamory 59593380 1.05 Bear in Big Blue House 18759380 1.35 Storylane 30101670 1.40 Barney 69097922 2.10 PICME 93852941 2.15 Pocoyo 45348583 2.25 Postman Pat 45335019 2.40 The Club: Harry 59354458 2.50 Gerald 59799100 3.10 My Life as a Teenage Robot 17515980 3.35 Yu-Gi-Oh 80725477 4.00 New Worst Witch 65331293 4.30 Sadie 65337477

5.00 Dustin's Daily News 39733699
5.20 news2day 89248293
5.35 TTV: Neighbours Robert leaves Paul to perish in a collapsing mineshaft. (S) 83977293
6.00 TTV: The Simpsons (S) 65341670
6.30 TTV: Home and Away Lucas is interrogated at the police station. (S) 65332922
7.00 Two Civilisation: Zero Hour "The Plot to Kill the Pope" 75670187
8.00 Who Betrayed Anne Frank? Biographer Carol Ann Lee examines clues about the three main suspects who might have revealed the Frank family's whereabouts to the Gestapo in 1944. 75689835
9.00 Scrubs Comedy. 46302854
9.30 Legend Drama series. Fridge is derailed by allegations of Harriet's infidelity. In his confusion, he acts rashly and pursues a new love interest. 31929380
10.30 Des Bishop: Joy in the Hood (R) 48517632
11.00 RTÉ News on Two and European Weather 46314699
11.30 24 "Day 5: 11.00pm to 12.00am" 93991922

12.25 Screen Two: Sunset Strip (2000) Comedy set in 1972. Over 24 hours a number of young artists, musicians and seekers of fame and fortune find their lives entangling in the sometimes sleazy heart of California's hippiest community. Anna Friel, Simon Baker. ★★★★★ 75927404 2.05 Viva la Bam A look at the chaotic life of Jackass star Bam Margera. 58481997 2.25 Nightscreen 22388220 5.00 Euro News 21466930

TG4

7.00 EuroNews 88203458 7.40 Doodlebops 62315800 8.05 Cúla 4 na nÓg 77841583 8.06 Tec an Tarracóir 68054093 8.20 Dor 89016019 8.45 Scéalta an Dragúin 72527583 9.00 Cedric 84234293 9.15 EuroNews 14989941 11.30 George Lopez 48510729 11.00 Comhraic (OS) 46386816 11.30 Two and a Half Men (TS) 26331458 11.55 An Aimsir Láithreach 89142125 12.00 Movie an Lae: Kiss Me Kate (1955) Starring Kathryn Grayson. A divorced pair of actors are brought together for a musical version of The Taming of the Shrew. ★★★★★ 23632632 2.00 Doodlebops 37833477 2.30 Cúla 4 11008309 2.31 Clifford 59700212 2.45 Baby Looney Tunes 59753545 3.15 Dora 14365467 3.40 What's New Scooby Doo? 80719816 4.05 Legend of the Dragon 97328106 4.30 Scil (OS) New Series Gaelic Games challenges. 65324903 5.00 Lizzie McGuire 39720125 5.20 Spongebob Squarepants 89242019 5.35 Sile 51447090 5.36 Pop 4 an tSamhraidh: Súil Siar (Repeat) 58200941

6.35 Stil na Réaltai: Charlize Theron 66576038
6.56 An Aimsir Láithreach 29313106
7.00 Nuacht TG4 95887835
7.22 An Aimsir Láithreach 57085699
7.30 SJAI Boswell Equestrian League 65325632
8.00 Comhrá: T.K. Whitaker (OS) New Series: T.K. Whitaker, former senator and civil servant, is Máirtín Tom Sheainín's guest . 37846941
8.30 GAA 2006 37832748
9.00 An Aimsir Láithreach 12919835
9.05 One Tree Hill (TS) Nathan and Lucas are influenced by the father of an old friend. 45936854
10.00 Cloch ar Chloch (OS) New Series: 10 people must leave their lives behind them when they decide to go trekking in Iceland for 3 weeks in an effort to lose weight. 48535038
10.30 Hector San Oz (OS) New Series Hector begins his journey around Australia in Sydney. 48511458
11.00 Without a Trace: A suspect goes berserk. 60527941

11.55 An Aimsir Láithreach 13805458 12.00 Behind the Mus 12.55 Scannán: The Enforcer (1976) Starring Clint Eastwood. Harry Callahan finds out his new partner is female. ★★★★★ 21988797 2.40 EuroNews 78999210

TV3

6.00 The Week in Review 69762545 6.30 Emmerdale 23636458 7.00 Ireland AM 86962274 10.00 Family Affairs 23650038 10.30 The Royal 77572106 11.30 Chef at Large 46385187 12.00 House Doctor Home improvements with real estate stylist Ann Maurice as she helps homeowners get their properties into saleable condition. 57265908 12.25 Family Affairs A lovelorn Jake has high hopes after his kiss with Lucy. With Ryan Davenport. 54015485 12.55 Ricki Lake 20822583 1.40 The Oprah Winfrey Show 57212403 2.35 All Saints Trish tells Nelson it is time he decided what he is going to do, making Kerry nervous. 51677361 3.30 Emmerdale Gray sets his sights on Mill Cottage. 65347854 4.00 Coronation Street Audrey calls on an old friend when faced with an emergency. Charlie tricks Tracy and plans a night of passion with Maria.65326361 4.30 Judge Judy Double bill of the show in which New York City's outspoken family court judge Judy Sheindlin presides over a series of real-life cases and conflicts. 16176854

5.30 News at 5.30 65346125
6.00 The Lion Man 65343038
6.30 News at 6.30 65327090
7.00 Emmerdale Perdy's horse has an accident while in Katie's care. 37835835
7.30 Coronation Street Shelley drops a bombshell on Bev. 65323274
8.00 Malcolm in the Middle One of Dewey's plans is foiled due to Tourette's. Reese discovers that Hal is prone to suggestion when sleepwalking. 37844583
8.30 Coronation Street Shelley's secret is out - but can a devastated Bev keep it to herself? 37823090
9.00 The Shield Vic learns that a Latino gang in prison has ordered the murders of two black victims on the outside. 75694767
10.00 Law and Order: SVU A student's claims of rape are brought into doubt when it is discovered she mothered two abandoned babies. 38765835
10.55 News Tonight 19433336
11.25 Eircom League Weekly 14439854

12.05 On the Limit Sports Motorsport action. 90020171 12.35 The Apprentice Reality TV series in which 14 candidates compete for the position of apprentice to multi-millionaire Sir Alan Sugar. 17834688 1.35 Ricki Lake Studio discussion. 36000607 5.50 Eircom League Weekly Trevor Welch presents highlights, previews, news and views on the Eircom League. 65715862

72 RTÉ GUIDE   Movie Ratings: ★★★★★Classic ★★★★★Excellent ★★★★★Good ★★★★★Fair ★★★★★Tragic   ★ = RTÉ Guide recommends

Practice questions

1. What programmes are scheduled for children?
2. What news programmes are shown?
3. How are teenagers catered for?
4. How would you improve this schedule?

Before you even look at an exam paper or textbook, you already know quite a lot about these two forms of media. You are exposed to them every day, but before you can answer a question on them, you need to be aware of a few key words:

- **National radio station:** A radio station that broadcasts to the whole country, e.g. Radio 1, 2FM and Today FM.
- **Local radio station:** A radio station that only broadcasts in a small location. They are mainly concerned with local events and provide a service to the local community, e.g. Clare FM, KFM, FM104.
- **Schedule:** The list of shows or programmes and the times they are broadcast. In a television schedule, the station will usually try to cater for the needs of the viewer at certain times. Children's programmes will be shown in the afternoon and more adult programmes later in the evening.
- **The watershed:** Before this time, usually 9.00 p.m., programmes must be suitable for family viewing. They should not contain violence or bad language.

Exam hints

Quite often in the exam you are asked to design you own advertisement, information leaflet, poster, etc. Your answer should be based on the key elements outlined on pp. 55–8. Divide your answer into the same sections as the question. When writing about how you would present your work, you could divide your answer into the written and visual parts of your design. For example, on the 2004 paper, students were asked to design a healthy living leaflet. The following sample answer shows how you could approach answering this question.

Sample question

You are preparing a leaflet on healthy living for distribution in your school.
1. Write out five points you would include in the leaflet.
2. Describe or illustrate how you would present these points on the page.

Sample answer

1. The five points I would have for my healthy living leaflet would be:
   (a) Exercise for an hour a day.
   (b) Eat five portions of fruit or vegetables a day.
   (c) Drink more water.
   (d) Cut down on sugary snacks and chocolate.
   (e) Always eat breakfast.

2. I would present these points in the following way:

   Written text

   My written text would have to be *eye catching*, so I would use a large font in red on a white background. My five points would be numbered. I would use a large tick or correct mark to the right of each point to remind people that this is the correct thing to do.

   Visuals

   The leaflet needs to make people aware of healthy living, so I would use very *vibrant, bright colours*. I would include a heart *logo*, as this is one of the most important aspects of the leaflet. I would get a celebrity to appear on the leaflet, as *celebrity endorsement* catches people's attention. I would use the *slogan* 'Your health is your wealth' – since this *rhymes*, it should be memorable. I would include smaller *photographs* of young people being active with happy, smiling faces, as this is our *target market*. I would use a plain white *background* to make all my main points stand out.

Chapter 5
Drama

This section is worth 60 marks. If this appears in section 4, it is compulsory. If it appears in section 5, 6 or 7, then you have a choice to answer two of the three sections on the paper.

This section begins with a piece of unseen drama that you must read. Questions A, B, C and D usually relate to the drama extract on the paper. These questions are usually worth 10 marks each. Your answers should be approximately 10 lines for each question and should include relevant quotation from the extract where necessary.

Question E usually relates to the play or film you have studied and is worth 20 marks. You should be able to write two or three paragraphs on the play or film you have studied.

UNSEEN DRAMA

Exam hints

- Read the **introduction** to the extract carefully, as it will give you information about the background to the piece and will probably explain who each of the characters are.
- Read the extract fully at least twice to make sure you understand what is taking place. Make sure you are aware of the key **characters** and their relationship to each other. What do they do or say in the extract that reveals their attitude towards each other?
- Take careful note of all the **stage directions**. These are usually in italics or in brackets and they tell you what the actors are doing at that time or how they say the lines.

- Take note of the description of the scene, as this will give you an idea of when and where the scene is **set**.

TYPES OF UNSEEN DRAMA QUESTIONS

In the Unseen Drama section, there are certain types of questions you may be asked.

Comprehension questions

This type of question tests how well you understand the passage. You may be asked what happened in the piece or what one character said or did. These questions are very straightforward. Answer them clearly and concisely, quoting from the extract to support your point. Make sure you use full sentences.

Character questions

You may be asked about a character from the text and what type of person they are. A character's personality is revealed through everything they **say** and **do.** Look at the lines that the character says – what do they tell you about the type of person he/she is? Also look at the stage directions, as they will tell you what the character does and can quite often tell you a lot more about the character.

Tone of voice questions

You may be asked what tone of voice a character would say a particular line in. In answering this question, look carefully at the stage directions, as they may already indicate how the line should be said. Also, look at what is happening in the scene at that time – for example, if the characters are having an argument, it is likely that any line would be delivered in an angry tone of voice. Try not to use the same words in your answer; there are more descriptive words than good, bad, happy or sad. Try to use words like excited, enthusiastic, frightened, scared, aggressive, coaxing, boasting, superior, hostile, forceful, assertive, insistent, nervous, timid, terrified, cheerful, delighted, miserable, depressing, gloomy, calm, outraged, annoyed, etc.

Dialogue questions

You may be asked to write the dialogue for the scene after the one given or for the one before. The dialogue need be no longer than 10 lines, so don't get caught up in your own story and write pages. Remember, you only have 25 minutes to do the entire drama section.

When writing dialogue, make sure you use the correct dialogue layout (the same as the dialogue on the paper) and use whatever information about the characters is given in the extract. Include your own stage directions if you wish using a different coloured pen or putting them in brackets. Look at the sample answer on p. 83 to see an example of dialogue.

Atmosphere questions

You may be asked how the writer creates a certain atmosphere in the piece, e.g. how she creates a sense of tension. To answer this question, look at what the characters do and say. The stage directions will give you an idea of what the audience would see and the lines the characters say should give you a sense of what the atmosphere is like.

Stagecraft questions

You will be asked about things that are specific to drama, e.g. set, costumes, props and direction.

Set

The set is whatever is on stage to tell the audience **where** the action is taking place. There may be a backdrop of a painted scene to give an illusion of depth to the stage, aspects of the scene may be painted onto flats (wooden cut-outs) at the side of the stage, or in some cases full replicas of rooms may be used on stage. The set can refer to the physical items on stage that give you a sense of place, including furniture, park benches, lamp posts, etc. Look

at the photo of a stage set and identify the things on stage that tell you when and where the play is set.

Costumes

The costumes are the clothes worn by the actor to give you a sense of character. We all make assumptions about people from the way they are dressed, so if you are asked to design the costume for a particular character, think about the image you want to portray. Are they old or young? Rich or poor? Scruffy or well dressed? Think not only about the clothes, but also the shoes and hairstyles of the characters, as they all give the audience an impression of the character. Look at the photograph of characters in costume. What type of people do you think they are? What gives you that impression of them?

Props

This is short for 'properties' and means anything else handled by the actors on the stage, such as telephones, guns, pens, books, cups, shovel, etc. They may be listed in the stage directions if they are vital to the story. Look at the photograph of a scene from a play. What items is the actor handling? These are the props.

Direction

You may be asked how you would direct a scene if you were the director. The director has complete control of the stage and it is his or her job to tell the actors where to move on stage and how to say their lines. As you read the piece, think about how you imagine it in your head. The director's job is to turn it into a reality by telling everyone else exactly what he or she wants them to do.

Sample question

Read the following extract, a scene adapted from Brian Friel's play, *Lovers*, taken from the 2005 exam, and examine the sample answers that follow.

Joe Brennan, aged seventeen and a half, and Mag Enright, aged seventeen, are sitting on a hilltop on a beautiful June morning. They have gone up there to study for their Leaving Certificate, which will begin in a few days. Joe and Mag are going to be married in three weeks' time.

Mag: I love the view of Ballymore from up here – the town, the lake, even the people. But when I'm down among them, I can't stand them. I bet that's how God feels at times too. Wouldn't you think so?

Joe: *(Trying to study)* I don't know how God feels.

Mag: Why not?

Joe: Because I'm not God.

Mag: Oh! You're so clever.

Joe: Look Mag, we came up here to study. What are you going to do first?

Mag: French. And then Maths and then Irish. And then English language and literature. After lunch Geography and History of the World. I have a planned programme for myself. What are you starting with?

Joe: Maths.

Mag: Then what?

Joe: That's all.

Mag: Only Maths?

Joe: Huh-huh.

Mag: Then, that's what I'll do too. *(Really worried)* My God, if the volume of a cone doesn't come up, I'm scootrified! Joe...

(Pause. There is silence for a few seconds)

Joe: What?

Mag: What's the difference between language and literature?

Joe: Stupid!

Mag: What?

Joe: (*Flings his book from him in annoyance*) You-are-a-bloody-pain-in-the-neck. You haven't shut up for a minute since we got here! You have done no work yourself and you have wasted my morning too! So, will you shut up!

Mag: (*With dignity*) I will. I certainly will. (*Brief pause*) But before I go silent for the rest of the day, there's something I want to get clear between us, Joe Brennan. (*Pause*) Joe, you never proposed to me.

Joe: Huh?

Mag: You haven't asked me to marry you. Our children will want to know. Especially the girls.

Joe: What are you raving about?

Mag: Propose to me!

Joe: God!

Mag: Now!

Joe: You really are...

Mag: Ask me!

Joe: Will-you-marry-me. Now!

Mag: Thank you, Joseph. I will.

Joe: Crazy! Absolutely, totally crazy!

A. In the last line, Joe tells Mag that she is 'Crazy! Absolutely, totally crazy!' Do you agree? Give reasons for your answer. (10)

B. How would you describe Joe's character? What does he say and do in this scene which leads you to this opinion of him? (10)

C. In what tone of voice do you think Joe speaks to Mag in this scene: Annoyed? Mocking? Loving? Amused? Give reasons for your choice. (10)

D. Imagine the scene where Mag announces to her parents that she and Joe are going to get married. Write the dialogue (about 10 lines) you think would have taken place between Mag and her parents. (10)

Sample answers

A. *In the last line, Joe tells Mag that she is 'Crazy! Absolutely, totally crazy!' Do you agree? Give reasons for your answer.* (10)

Yes, I agree that Mag in this extract seems to be crazy. Firstly, she lists off all the subjects she is going to study but she changes her mind instantly when she hears that Joe is only doing Maths: 'Then, that's what I'll do too.' She then keeps asking him silly questions and eventually wants him to propose to her because their 'children will want to know'. This seems to be very crazy behaviour, so I agree with Joe that Mag is totally crazy.

B. *How would you describe Joe's character? What does he say and do in this scene which leads you to this opinion of him?* (10)

I think Joe is a very serious character in this extract. All he wants to do is study his Maths and Mag keeps annoying him: 'Look Mag, we came up here to study.' I also think he is not very patient and is very easily annoyed. He calls Mag 'a- bloody-pain-in-the-neck' when she asks him a question about language and literature. But I think he really does like Mag, as he does ask her to marry him when she keeps asking him to: 'Will-you-marry-me.'

C. *In what tone of voice do you think Joe speaks to Mag in this scene: Annoyed? Mocking? Loving? Amused? Give reasons for your choice.* (10)

I think Joe speaks to Mag in a very annoyed tone of voice. From the beginning he is trying to study and she keeps interrupting him, so all his lines are very short, such as 'That's all.' I also think Joe speaks in an annoyed tone because the stage directions tell us that he 'flings his book from him in annoyance'. Lastly, the writer uses hyphens between the words to show that they are said in a very annoyed or staccato tone: 'You-are-a-bloody-pain-in-the-neck'.

D. *Imagine the scene where Mag announces to her parents that she and Joe are going to get married. Write the dialogue (about 10 lines) you think would have taken place between Mag and her parents.* (10)

Mag: Mam, Dad, I've got something to tell you.

Mam: What, love?

Mag: I think you should sit down.

Dad: Why? What is it? What's wrong?

Mag: Nothing's wrong, Dad! It's the best news in the world! Joe and I are going to get married!

Dad: What?

Mam: What do you mean? You're too young to get married!

Mag: But we're in love, Mam!

Dad: I don't care what you think you are! You are too young to get married and that's the end of it!

Mag: You can't stop us! We love each other and we are going to get married! *(She storms out the door)*

Practice questions

Read this scene, adapted for the 2004 exam paper from *Just the Job* by Ann Farquhar-Smith, and answer the questions which follow.

Jason O'Reilly has an appointment for an interview with the Personnel Manager at Jackson's. Before the interview, there is a discussion at home with his family.

Scene I: The O'Reilly Home

Jason: Mom! I've got an appointment for an interview with the Personnel Manager at Jackson's on Tuesday.

Mrs O'Reilly: Well done, Jason. An interview means you've nearly got the job.

Mr O'Reilly: But he hasn't yet, has he?

Mrs O'Reilly: Appearance is most important at an interview, Jason. You'd better think about what you're going to wear.

Mr O'Reilly: Your Mother's right. You'll need to wear a suit.

Jason: But I haven't got a suit.

Mrs O'Reilly: Yes, you have. There's the one you wore to your Aunt Kate's wedding.

Jason: That won't fit me. I've grown a bit since then.

Mrs O'Reilly: I can let it out. You've not grown that much.

Julie (Jason's sister): And you'll have to get your hair cut, and get rid of that earring.

Jason: Why? I'm not joining the army. I want a job as a fitter.

Mrs O'Reilly: Your sister is right, Jason. You've let your hair get out of hand since you left school and that earring does nothing for your image.

Jason: What image? I like my hair like this and earrings are the fashion.

Mr O'Reilly: You may like your hair and that filthy looking stud, but the Personnel Manager won't.

Jason: I'd rather draw the dole than have a short back and sides.

Mr O'Reilly: You can let it grow again after the interview.

Jason: I'm not applying to be Managing Director, you know, Dad! Have I got to go to all this trouble?

Julie: Why can't you make an effort to do the right thing for once?

> Mr O'Reilly: With jobs as scarce as they are nowadays, nothing should be too much trouble.
>
> Jason: And nothing is what I'd like to do!

Questions

1. What advice is Jason getting at home about his interview? (10)
2. From what you read in this piece, would you give the job to Jason? Explain your answer. (10)
3. Imagine that you are the costume designer for this play. Describe the costume you would design for **ONE** of the following characters: Mr O' Reilly, Mrs O' Reilly or Julie. Say why you have chosen your design. (10)
4. Imagine **Scene II, The Interview**. Write an opening dialogue (about 10 lines) between the Personnel Manager and Jason. (10)

STUDIED DRAMA

The last question in the Drama section asks you about a play or film you have studied. This question is worth 20 marks and should take you about 10 minutes to write. That means that you should be able to write at least three paragraphs on your play or film.

From your play or film you should know the following:

- **Key character:** Describe the central character in the play or film. How have they changed during the play or film? Describe a key moment in the play or film that changed them.
- **Key scene:** Describe exactly what happens in a key scene in the play or film. Who was involved in the scene? Why was the scene so important? Does it change the outcome of the play or film? How?
- **Moment of conflict:** Describe a scene in the play or film with conflict. Who was involved? Why did the conflict arise? How was it resolved? What happened then? Was there tension? How was this created?

Exam hints

- The first line of your answer should state the name of the play you have studied and the author, or in the case of a film, the name of the film and the writer or director, so learn to spell the names correctly. For example, 'The play I have studied is *The Field* by John B. Keane.'
- Don't just write about a film you saw recently. You may not know the names of the characters, the director or the place it is set.
- Break your answer down into paragraphs. These should answer each part of the question separately. For example, a question that asks you to 'describe a scene, explain how the conflict was created and say how it was resolved' should be broken into three separate paragraphs.
- Practise writing about the key scenes and characters before the exam.

Sample question

The following is a key scene from the play *Our Day Out* by Willy Russell (Menthuen, 1984). Read the scene and the sample answer below. Then, using the play you have studied, attempt the questions that follow.

In this play, a group of children from Mrs Kay's progress class are brought on a day trip to Conway Castle in Wales. The children are from the backstreets of Liverpool and this trip is a new experience for many of them. One of the children, Carol, doesn't want to return home to her depressing life after the trip. Mr Briggs, a teacher reluctantly on the trip who doesn't like the children very much, finds her and has to persuade her to come back.

Briggs: Carol Chandler, just come here. Who gave you permission to come on these cliffs?
Carol *(moving to the edge):* No one.
She turns and dismisses him.
Briggs: I'm talking to you Miss Chandler.
She continues to ignore his presence.
Now just listen here young lady...
Carol *(suddenly turning):* Don't you come near me!
Briggs *(taken aback by her vehemence, he stops):* Pardon?
Carol: I don't want you to come near me.

Briggs: Well in that case just get yourself moving and let's get down to the beach.

Carol: You go. I'm not coming.

Briggs: You what?

Carol: Tell Mrs Kay she can go home without me. I'm stoppin' here by the sea.

Pause.

Briggs: Now you just listen to me. I've had just about enough and I'm not putting up with a pile of silliness from the likes of you. Now come on!

He starts towards her but she moves to the very edge of the cliff.

Carol: Try an' get me an' I'll jump over.

Briggs stops in his tracks, astounded and angered.

Briggs *(shouting)*: Listen you stupid girl, get yourself over here this minute.

She ignores him.

I'll not tell you again!

They stare at each other. It's obvious that she will not do as he bids.

I'll give you five seconds! Just five seconds. One, two, three, four, I'm warning you!...Five.

Carol: I've told y', I'm not comin' with y'. I will jump y' know. I will.

Briggs: Just what are you tryin' to do to me?

Carol: I've told y', just leave me alone an' I won't jump. *(Pause)* I wanna stay here where it's nice.

Briggs: Stay here? How could you stay here? What would you do eh? Where would you live?

Carol: I'd be alright.

Briggs: I've told you, stop being silly.

Carol *(turning on him)*: What are you worried for eh? You don't care do y'? Do y'?

Briggs: What? About you?...Listen, if I didn't care, why would I be up here now, trying to stop you doing something stupid?

Carol: Because if I jumped over, you'd get into trouble when you get back to school. That's why Briggsy, so stop goin' on. You hate me.

Briggs: Don't be ridiculous. Just because I'm a schoolteacher it doesn't mean to say that...

Carol: Don't lie, you! I know you hate me. I've seen you goin' home in your car, passin' us on the street. An' the way you look at us. You hate all the kids.

Briggs: What...why do you say that?

Carol: Why can't I just stay out here an' live in one of them nice white houses, an' do the garden an' that?

Briggs: Look...Carol...You're talking as though life for you is ending, instead of just beginning. Now why can't...I mean, if that's what you want...why can't...what's to stop you working hard at school from now on, getting a good job and then moving out here when you're old enough? Eh?

Carol *(she turns and looks at him with pure contempt):* Don't be so bloody stupid.

She turns to look out to the sea.

It's been a great day today. I loved it. I don't wanna leave here an' go home. (*Pause*) If I stayed it wouldn't be any good though, would it? You'd send the coppers to get me, wouldn't y'?

Briggs: We'd have to. How would you survive out here?

Carol: I know. (*Pause*) I'm not goin' back though.

She kneels at the cliff edge, looks over.

Briggs: Carol...please...

Carol: Sir...you know if you'd been my old feller...I would've been all right wouldn't I?

Briggs slowly and cautiously creeping forward, holding out his hand.

Briggs: Carol, please come away from there.

She looks down over the cliff.

Please.

Carol: Sir...sir you don't half look funny y' know.

Briggs *(smiling):* Why?

Carol: Sir, you should smile more often. You look great when y' smile.

Briggs *(holding out his hand):* Come on, Carol.

Carol: Sir...what'll happen to me for doin' this?

Briggs: Nothin'...I promise.

Carol: Sir, you're promisin' now, but what about back at school?

Briggs: It won't even be mentioned, I promise...

His hand outstretched. She decides to believe him. She reaches out for his hand. As she does she slips but he manages to lunge forward and clasp her to safety.

From a play or film you have studied, describe a scene which had you on the edge of your seat. Say how and why you found the scene tense and exciting. You must name the play or the film you have studied. (2000)

Sample answer

The play I have studied is *Our Day Out* by Willy Russell. In this play a group of school children go on a school trip to Conway Castle. The play is set in Liverpool and the children are from the progress class. They have never been away before and cause chaos wherever they go.

One of the children, Carol, didn't want to go home. The scene that had me on the edge of my seat was when Carol was on the cliff threatening to jump. Mr Briggs, the grumpy, strict teacher, told her she was being silly and that she had to go home. Carol said she didn't want to go back there and she moved closer to the edge.

I found this scene tense and exciting because you don't know what is going to happen next. Mr Briggs tried to force her to come down by counting to five, but Carol didn't move. This made it very exciting as you want to see what he will do next.

Mr Briggs promised her that he wouldn't say anything to the others and Carol moved towards him but she slipped and Mr Briggs had to catch her to stop her from falling off the cliff. This created tension in the scene.

For these reasons this scene had me on the edge of my seat.

ANSWERING ON A FILM

When answering this question on a film you have studied, you need to be aware of the same aspects of the film as of the play, e.g. characters, key scenes, moments of conflict.

Make sure you don't just rewrite the entire plot of the film. You are asked a specific question on a scene or a character and you must limit your answer to that question. Make sure you know the name of the director of the film.

Practice questions

1. Name a play or a film you have studied. Pick the scene you remember best from the play or film and write about:
   - What exactly happened.
   - How any one character behaved.
   - What especially makes you remember the scene you have chosen. (2005)

2. Name a play or film you have studied. Using **ONE** of the following headings, write about the play or film:
   - The scene I liked best.
   - The character I found most interesting.
   - Why I found the play/film enjoyable.
   - Why I did not enjoy the play/film. (2004)

3. Think about a play or film you have studied. Pick a very dramatic moment from it and write about:
   - What exactly happened.
   - Which characters were involved.
   - How any one character behaved. (2002)

4. From a play or film you have studied, describe a scene:
   - Where **one person** behaves in a way that another person does not like.
     OR
   - Where a **group of people** behave in a way that another group of people does not like.

   Whose side were you on in that scene? Explain why. (2001)

Chapter 6
Poetry

WHAT IS POETRY?

Poetry is a picture in words. The poet tries to capture a moment, memory or an event in words. The words he or she chooses are important, as every word has meaning and is chosen for a reason. Like an artist, the poet may use certain techniques to describe the scene, such as imagery or comparison.

But as well as creating a visual picture, poetry uses another sense as well as vision – sound. The poet knows how certain words sound and uses these sounds to create rhythm and rhyme in the poem.

In the exam, you must examine the poetry on the paper and respond to it, giving your own point of view, and comment on the poetry you have previously studied.

THE EXAM PAPER

In the Junior Certificate exam, the questions in the poetry section are based on an unseen poem and the poetry you have studied. The entire section is worth 60 marks – 40 for your answers on the unseen poem and 20 for the poetry you have studied throughout the year. As with each section of this paper, you have approximately **25 minutes** to read and answer each section. If poetry is in section 4 of the exam, then it must be answered.

UNSEEN POETRY

You are asked to read a poem and answer the questions that follow.

Exam hints

- Read the title of the poem carefully! This could give you a sense of what the poem is about.
- Read the poem slowly. Make sure you understand what happens in the poem. Don't jump to conclusions.
- Reread the poem. Identify any words or phrases that stand out.

Poetry checklist

In the exam you will be tested on your understanding of the poem, so ask yourself the following questions as you read the poem.

- **Who** is speaking in the poem? Does the poet use the word 'I'? Is the poet pretending to be someone else? Is the poet writing about someone else?
- **What** happens in the poem? Look out for key action words or verbs that describe what happens, e.g. 'I went', 'She cried', 'I wandered'.
- **When** does the poem take place? Does the poet mention a time of day or night? Is it winter or summer? Does the poet give us any clues about the season?
- **Where** is the poem set? Does the poet mention places or describe the environment?

Once you know the answers to these questions, you can then look at **how** the poet tells us his or her story.

How does the poet **feel**? The poet's feelings or the mood of the poem is often shown or conveyed by the words the poet chooses. No word in a poem is just there by chance. The poet has taken his/her time and chosen the words that **best describe** the feeling he/she wanted to convey or show. It is up to you to look at the words in the poem and decide what the poet was trying to convey.

What is the **mood** or **atmosphere** of the poem? Again, the words chosen by the poet tell us the mood of the poem. Is the poem optimistic or pessimistic? Does the poet use dark, depressing imagery or bright, joyful words and phrases?

Look at the following lines and assess the feelings and mood of the poet.

- 'Around the gable-end a starved wind razors and from the split gutters icicles hang like fangs.' ('Visitor' by Wes Magee)

- 'When all at once I saw a crowd, a host of golden daffodils; Beside the lake beneath the trees fluttering and dancing in the breeze.' ('I wandered lonely as a cloud' by William Wordsworth)

Both poems describe the wind, but the words chosen by each poet create a very different atmosphere or mood in the poem.

In the first poem, the poet uses words like *starved*, *razors* and *fangs*. All of these words are negative and make the wind seem harsh and cruel. In the second poem, the poet uses words that are gentle and positive, such as *fluttering* and *dancing*. This creates a calm, peaceful atmosphere.

What **words** or **phases** stand out in the poem? Poets use certain techniques in their poetry. It is up to you to identify these techniques and comment on them in your answers.

Alliteration: *Words that begin with the same letter*

Examples: **Kn**ock-**kn**eed
             Forest's **f**erny **f**loor,
             Watch the **w**hite eyes **w**rithing

The poet uses alliteration to add **emphasis** to the poem, to draw the reader's attention to a certain point or to create certain sounds in the poem. Some letters create soft sounds and so have a calming effect, while others are quite harsh and create a negative, grating sound.

Repeatedly using the letter 's' has a special name – **sibilance**. Sibilance is used regularly in poetry to create a soft, gentle sound, e.g. 'Snowdrops and candles soothed the bedside', 'Silence surged softly'.

Assonance: *Words that use the same vowel sounds*

Examples: M**oo**nlit d**oo**r
             Cl**i**pped s**i**des

The poet uses assonance to speed up or slow down the line. In general, broad vowels (a, o, u) tend to slow down the line and make the line seem more sad, e.g. 'f**o**re bem**oa**ned m**oa**n', but the slender vowels (i, e) tend to quicken the line and make the poem seem more lively.

Simile: A comparison using the words 'like' or 'as'

Examples: His face was **as** white **as** snow.

The playground emptied just **as** though a plug was pulled.

The poet uses similes to expand on the images created in the poem. This helps us to imagine exactly what the poet wants us to see.

Metaphor: A comparison not using the words 'like' or 'as'

Examples: Our yells were wolves howling.

The sea is a hungry dog.

The poet uses metaphors to make the comparison more dramatic.

Ononatopaoea — word sounds like it means.

Repetition: Repeating a word or phrase

Examples: 'Gas! Gas! Quick boys!'

'Looking for you and me, my dear, looking for you and me.'

The poet uses repetition to make a moment more dramatic, urgent or sad.

Other aspects of poetry that you should be able to comment on are:
- **Imagery:** The words or phrases that create pictures in your head.
- **Rhyme:** The words that rhyme in the poem. They may be close together and regular, or far apart and irregular. Look at what effect this has on the poem.
- **Rhythm:** This is the rhythm or beat created by the sounds of the words as they are said aloud. The rhythm may change in a poem and it usually reflects the mood, e.g. a quick, lively rhythm reflects a bright, happy mood.
- **Language:** Look at the types of words used by the poet. Does the poet use unusual words? Are slang words used or does the poet stick to formal language?

EXAM QUESTIONS ON THE UNSEEN POEM

The following are the types of question you may be asked in the unseen poetry section of the paper:

- Where does the poem take place?
- Why does the poet make this comparison?
- What were the reactions of the people in the poem?
- Name two things the poet notices.
- What is your favourite word or image from the poem?
- What sort of person is the poet?
- Give two reasons why you think this poem deserved a prize.
- Who is speaking in the poem?
- How does the person in the poem feel?
- What happens in the poem?
- What time of year do you think this takes place?
- Why do you think the poet uses this title for the poem?

In the exam, the first three or four questions are based on the poem printed on the paper. These questions are worth 40 marks in total.

The last question relates to the poetry you have studied. This question is worth 20 marks.

Make sure you answer the questions according to the marks awarded for them. In other words, you should spend twice as much time on a 20 mark question as you spend on a 10 mark question.

HOW TO ANSWER THE EXAM QUESTION

- Read the question carefully. Underline the key words in the question.
- Use full sentences.
- Use the key words from the question in your answer.
- Use quotes from the poem on the paper to prove your point.
- Don't misspell words that are printed on the paper.
- Write according to the marks allowed, e.g. a 10 mark question requires eight to ten lines in your answer, but a 5 mark question only requires one or two sentences.

Sample questions

AN AFRICAN THUNDERSTORM
by David Rubadiri (adapted for the 2005 exam paper)

1 From the west
Clouds come hurrying with the wind
Turning
Sharply
Here and there
Whirling
Like a madman chasing nothing.
The Wind whistles by
And trees bend to let it pass.

2 In the village
Screams of delighted children
Toss and turn
In the din of the whirling wind,
Women –
Babies clinging on their backs –
Dart about
In and out
Madly.
The Wind whistles by
While trees bend to let it pass.

3 Clothes wave like torn flags
As zig-zag blinding flashes
Rumble, tremble, and crack
Amidst the smell of fired smoke
And the pelting march of the storm.

A. (i)   Where is the storm coming from?   (5)
    (ii) With what is the storm compared in stanza 1?   (5)

B. In stanza 2, how do:
    (i) The children react to the approaching storm?   (5)
    (ii) The women react to the approaching storm?   (5)

C. In stanza 3, is the storm described as being:
    exciting? **OR** frightening? **OR** violent? Give reasons for your answer.   (10)

D. Which line in the poem gives us the best idea of the wind's speed?
    Give reasons for your answer.   (10)

E. Think about poems you have studied and choose one which best describes
    an exciting person **OR** an exciting event.
    • Name the poem and the poet.
    • What is the poem about?
    • What is special about the exciting person **OR** event in this poem
      which makes you remember it so well?   (20)

(taken from the 2005 Junior Certificate exam)

Sample answers

Questions A, B, C and D are based on the poem printed on the paper. Question E
relates to your studied poetry.

Exam hints
• Divide your answers the same way the questions are divided up. This
  gives the examiner a chance to give you marks for each section. If you
  stick all your answers together, it is harder for them to give you marks.
  Always label the answer clearly.
• Always use full sentences!

Questions

A. (i) *Where is the storm coming from?*   *(5)*
         The storm is coming from the west, as the poet says 'From the west
         clouds come hurrying with the wind'.

(ii)   *With what is the storm compared in stanza 1?*   *(5)*
In the first stanza, the storm is compared to a madman. The poet says that the wind was 'like a madman chasing nothing'.

B.   *In stanza 2, how do:*
(i)   *The children react to the approaching storm?*   *(5)*
(ii)   *The women react to the approaching storm?*   *(5)*

(i)   The children react to the approaching storm by screaming, but they do not seem to be frightened, as they are described as 'delighted children'.

(ii)   The women react to the approaching storm by rushing about. They seem to be very busy as they 'dart about in and out madly'. They also have to look after the younger children, as they have 'babies clinging on their backs'.

At least two reasons given, supported by quotes.

C.   *In stanza 3, is the storm described as being: exciting?* **OR** *frightening?*
OR *violent? Give reasons for your answer.*   *(10)*
I think the storm is described as both frightening and violent in stanza 3. The poet uses words like 'torn', 'blinding', 'rumble, tremble and crack' to describe the terrifying effects of the storm. The description also sounds like a battlefield when he says 'the smell of fired smoke' and the 'pelting march of the storm'.

D.   *Which line in the poem gives us the best idea of the wind's speed? Give reasons for your answer.*   *(10)*
'The wind whistles by while trees bend to let it pass'. I think this line shows the speed of the wind. The poet uses **alliteration** in this line when he repeats the letter 'w'. I think this speeds up the line and imitates the sound of the wind. By using the word 'whistled', it makes the wind sound like a train and gives us an idea of the wind's speed. The poet also uses **repetition**, as this line is repeated at the end of the first and second stanzas.

At least two reasons given and key words used.

Practice questions

THE OLD LADY
by Robert Adcock
(adapted for the Junior Certificate 2004 exam)

The day we went bob-a-jobbing
We met her.
She sat there
In a dainty old chair.
She never moved,
Her faint hands
Perched on the chair
Like two shot birds.
She was wrapped head to foot
In blankets and shawls
As if she was a hermit crab
In her neutral home.

Wrinkles curved over her soft face
As if a snail had left its trail.
She opened her mouth
and mumbled, 'Hello'.
She looked pleased with herself
Like a child who had just
Learnt to write her name.
Her hair —
What was left of it —
Looked like tiny spiders' webs
Knotting all over.

She took my hand
As if to say, 'Come closer'.
She felt my face
As if wondering whether to buy me or not.
She clutched my hand harder,
Then let go.

I sniffed a pricey perfume
Over her clingfilm skin.
Then with a great sigh
She leaned back into her chair.
I knew then, it was time to go.

Questions

A.   This poem, by Robert Adcock, describes an old lady. Name two things
      he noticed about her when he first met her.   (10)

B.   What is your favourite word or image from the poem? Explain why. (10)

C.   From your reading of this poem, what sort of person do you think
      the poet, Robert Adcock, is?   (10)

D.   This is a prize-winning poem from a collection called *Young Words*.
      Give two reasons why you think this poem won a prize.   (10)

VISITOR
by Wes Magee

Sliding in slippers along the house-side
You find fragments of the turkey's carcass*   *Skeleton
Beside the toppled dustbin lid, and there
On the lawn's snow quilt, a line of paw marks.

Town fox, that wraith* of winter, soundlessly   *ghost
Thieved here as frost bit hard and stars shivered.
This bleak morning, under a raw-boned sky,
You stoop to examine the frozen tracks.

And print yours where a spectral* guest came late   *ghostly
To share a Christmas dinner. Around the
Gable-end a starved wind razors and from
The split gutters icicles hang like fangs.

Questions

A. In your own words, briefly describe what happens in the poem. Your description should be about six lines of your answer book in length. (10)

B. From your reading of the entire poem (title and text), how would you describe the poet's feelings towards the fox? Give reasons for your answer. (10)

C. Examine the first line of stanza 1 carefully: 'Sliding in slippers along the house-side'. What sound is most obvious in the line? Why do you think this sound is used? (10)

D. From either stanza 1 or stanza 2, pick one phrase you found particularly descriptive and say why you chose it. (10)

STUDIED POETRY

To prepare for this section of the paper, you should make sure that you have an adequate selection of poetry to answer the questions asked.

You are asked to choose a poem that you have studied that matches a heading given. You are generally asked to:

- Name the poem and poet.
- Describe what happens in the poem.
- Outline your reasons for liking/disliking the poem.
- Comment on some aspect of the poem.

Typical headings given are:

- A poem that describes an exciting person or event.
- Any poem that deserved a prize.
- A poem that made you sad or angry.
- A poem that created a clear picture in your head.
- A poem that described people, animals, nature, weather, a place, etc.
- A poem that made you feel happiness or joy.
- A poem that describes a memory.

To prepare for the exam, you should be able to write three paragraphs on your studied poems, outlining what happens in the poem, your reasons for liking/disliking the poem and a comment on some aspect of the poem, e.g. how it made you feel.

Sample poetry

The following is a selection of poetry you may use for your studied poetry section. To prepare for your exam, you should be able to answer the questions that follow each poem.

Key themes: childhood, memories, death, sadness, event

MID-TERM BREAK
by Seamus Heaney

I sat all morning in the college sick bay
Counting bells knelling classes to a close.
At two o'clock our neighbours drove me home.
In the porch I met my father crying –
He had always taken funerals in his stride –
And Big Jim Evans saying it was a hard blow.
The baby cooed and laughed and rocked the pram
When I came in, and I was embarrassed
By old men standing up to shake my hand
And tell me they were 'sorry for my trouble',
Whispers informed strangers I was the eldest,
Away at school, as my mother held my hand
In hers and coughed out angry tearless sighs.
At ten o'clock the ambulance arrived
With the corpse, stanched and bandaged by the nurses.
Next morning I went up into the room. Snowdrops
And candles soothed the bedside; I saw him
For the first time in six weeks. Paler now,
Wearing a poppy bruise on his left temple,
He lay in the four foot box as in his cot.
No gaudy scars, the bumper knocked him clear.
A four foot box, a foot for every year.

Questions

1. Describe what happens in the poem.
2. How did this poem make you feel?
3. What words or phrases in the poem stand out? Why?
4. Pick out examples of alliteration, repetition, assonance and simile.

Key themes: nature, youth, memories, growing up, event

THE EARLY PURGES

by Seamus Heaney

I was six when I first saw kittens drown
Dan Taggart pitched them, the scraggy wee shits
Into a bucket: a frail metal sound
Soft paws scraping like mad. But their tiny din
Was soon soused. They were slung on the snout
Of the pump and the water pumped in
'Sure isn't it better for them now?' Dan said.
Like wet gloves they bobbed and shone till he sluiced
Them out on the dunghill, glossy and dead
Suddenly frightened, for days I sadly hung
Round the yard, watching the three sogged remains
Turn mealy and crisp as old summer dung
Until I forgot them. But the fear came back
When Dan trapped big rats, snared rabbits, shot crows
Or, with a sickening tug, pulled old hens' necks,
Still, living displaces false sentiments
And now, when shrill pups are prodded to drown
I just shrug. 'Bloody pups.' It makes sense:
'Prevention of cruelty' talk cuts ice in town
Where they consider death unnatural —
But on well-run farms pests have to be kept down.

Questions

1. Describe what happens in the poem.
2. How do you feel having read the poem?
3. What words or phrases in the poem stand out? Why?

4.   What does the poet say about nature?
5.   Compare the two poems by Seamus Heaney. How are they similar? How are they different?
6.   Which one do you prefer? Why?

Key themes: war, death, sadness, anger, event

DULCE ET DECORUM EST
by Wilfred Owen

Bent double, like old beggars under sacks,
Knock-kneed, coughing like hags, we cursed through the sludge,
Till on the haunting flares we turned our backs,
And towards our distant rest began to trudge.
Men marched asleep. Many had lost their boots
But limped on, blood-shod. All went lame; all blind;
Drunk with fatigue; deaf even to the hoots
Of tired, outstripped Five-nines that dropped behind.

Gas! Gas! Quick, boys! – An ecstasy of fumbling,
Fitting the clumsy helmets just in time;
But someone still was yelling out and stumbling,
And flound'ring like a man in fire or lime...
Dim, through the misty panes and thick green light,
As under a green sea, I saw him drowning.
In all my dreams, before my helpless sight,
He plunges at me, guttering, choking, drowning.

If in some smothering dreams, you too could pace
Behind the wagon that we flung him in,
And watch the white eyes writhing in his face,
His hanging face, like a devil's sick of sin;
If you could hear, at every jolt, the blood
Come gargling from the froth-corrupted lungs,
Obscene as cancer, bitter as the cud
Of vile, incurable sores on innocent tongues –
My friend, you would not tell with such high zest

To children ardent for some desperate glory,
The old Lie: *Dulce et decorum est*
*Pro patria mori.**

*It is good and honourable to die for your country

Questions

1. Describe in detail what happens in the poem.
2. How does the poet describe the death of the soldier?
3. What comparisons (similes and metaphors) does the poet use in the poem?
4. Why do you think the poet uses them?
5. What words or phrases stand out in the poem?
6. What do you think the poet's attitude to war is? Give reasons for your answer.

Key themes: nature, happiness, event

I WANDERED LONELY AS A CLOUD
by William Wordsworth

I wandered lonely as a cloud
That floats on high o'er vales and hills,
When all at once I saw a crowd,
A host of golden daffodils;
Beside the lake, beneath the trees,
Fluttering and dancing in the breeze.

Continuous as the stars that shine
And twinkle on the Milky Way,
They stretched in never-ending line
Along the margin of a bay:
Ten thousand saw I at a glance,
Tossing their heads in sprightly dance.

The waves beside them danced; but they
Outdid the sparkling waves in glee:
A poet could not but be gay,
In such a jocund company:
I gazed – and gazed – but little thought
What wealth the show to me had brought:

For oft, when on my couch I lie
In vacant or in pensive mood,
They flash upon that inward eye
Which is the bliss of solitude;
And then my heart with pleasure fills,
And dances with the daffodils.

Questions

1. Describe what happens in the poem.
2. What words in the poem show the poet's happiness?
3. What words or images from the poem stand out? Why?
4. What is the poet's attitude towards nature?

Key themes: mystery, event, describing a scene

THE LISTENERS
by Walter de la Mare

"Is there anybody there?" said the Traveller,
Knocking on the moonlit door:
And his horse in the silence champed the grasses
Of the forest's ferny floor:
And a bird flew up out of the turret,
Above the Traveller's head:
And he smote upon the door again a second time;
"Is there anybody there?" he said.
But no one descended to the Traveller;
No head from the leaf-fringed sill
Leaned over and looked into his grey eyes,
Where he stood perplexed and still.

But only a host of phantom listeners
That dwelt in the lone house then
Stood listening in the quiet of the moonlight
To that voice from the world of men:
Stood thronging the faint moonbeams on the dark stair,
That goes down to the empty hall,
Hearkening in an air stirred and shaken
By the lonely Traveller's call.
And he felt in his heart their strangeness,
Their stillness answering his cry,
While his horse moved, cropping the dark turf,
'Neath the starred and leafy sky;
For he suddenly smote on the door, even
Louder, and lifted his head: —
"Tell them I came, and no one answered,
That I kept my word," he said.
Never the least stir made the listeners,
Though every word he spake
Fell echoing through the shadowiness of the still house
From the one man left awake:
Ay, they heard his foot upon the stirrup,
And the sound of iron on stone,
And how the silence surged softly backward,
When the plunging hoofs were gone.

Questions

1. Describe what happens in the poem.
2. How does the poet create a sense of mystery?
3. The poet uses a lot of sibilance (repeated use of 's' sound). What effect does that have on the poem?
4. What words does the poet use that shows that this poem was written a long time ago?

Key themes: childhood, school, conflict

FIGHT!
by Barrie Wade

'A scrap! A scrap!'
The tingle in the scalp
starts us running.

The shout drains
our playground just as though
a plug was pulled

here in the space
in which two twisted, furious
bodies writhe.

Rules will not prise
these savages apart.
No ref will interpose

with shouts of 'Break!'
This contest has one single
vicious round

of grab and grapple,
wrestle, thump and scrabble,
flail and scratch.

We take no sides.
Our yells are wolves howling
for blood of any kind.

Our fingers clench.
The thrill claws our throats
like raging thirst.

The whistle shrills
and splits our pack. The circle
heaves and shatters.

The fighters still
are blind and deaf, won't hear
or see until,

parted, they go limp
as cubs drawn by the scruff
from some hot lair.

Now they are tame,
Standing outside Sir's room
grinning their shame.

Chastened, we feel
the snarls of wildness
stifle in us.

Questions

1. What happens in the poem?
2. How does the poet make the boys sound like animals?
3. How does the crowd react?
4. Pick an image you like from the poem and explain why you like it.
5. The poet uses many similes and metaphors. Give examples from the poem.

Key themes: love, loss, memories

IN MY LIFE
Lennon and McCartney

There are places I'll remember
All my life though some have changed
Some forever not for better
Some have gone and some remain
All these places have their moments

With lovers and friends
I still can recall
Some are dead and some are living
In my life I've loved them all

But of all these friends and lovers
There is no one compares with you
And these memories lose their meaning
When I think of love as something new

Though I know I'll never lose affection
For people and things that went before
I know I'll often stop
And think about them
In my life I love you more

Though I know I'll never lose affection
For people and things that went before
I know I'll often stop
And think about them
In my life I love you more
In my life I love you more

Questions

1. What does the poet feel in this poem/lyric?
2. How does he show his feelings?
3. Pick a line from the poem that you like and explain why.

Exam hints

- When answering the last question in the poetry section, you may use some of the poetry above or other poetry you have studied during the year.
- Your first sentence should name the poem and poet you are focusing on.
- Know how to spell the names of the poems and poets!
- Clearly state what theme you are talking about.

- Use quotations from the poems to support your points – memorise quotes from each poem.
- Use the poetry checklist on pages 92–94 to make sure you know the studied poetry.
- Divide your answer into paragraphs; use the divisions in the question.
- Be able to summarise the poem in a paragraph.
- Be able to give reasons why you like the poem.
- It is easier to be positive in your answer – saying you don't like the poem leaves you with nothing to say. Your aim is to pick up marks, not throw them away!

Sample question

E.   Think about poems you have studied and choose one which best describes an exciting person **OR** an exciting event.
- Name the poem and the poet.
- What is the poem about?
- What is special about the exciting person **OR** event in this poem which makes you remember it so well? (20 marks, 2005)

Sample answer

The poem that I have studied that describes an exciting event is 'Dulce et Decorum est' by Wilfred Owen.

In this poem, Owen describes his experience in World War One. The event he describes is when he and his comrades are on their way back from the frontline when they are attacked with mustard gas and one of the soldiers dies. He describes in detail what happened to the man and how he has had nightmares ever since about the man 'guttering, choking, drowning'.

I remember this event very well because the descriptions he uses are so vivid. He uses a simile to describe the gas, 'as under a green sea', and describes the reactions of the men by using repetition, 'Gas! Gas! Quick, boys!' He uses a number of similes to show how distressing the scene was, 'obscene as cancer', 'bitter as the cud'. I also find the event easy to remember as he is very passionate at the end of the poem when he says 'My friend, you would not tell with such high zest/To children ardent for some desperate glory,/The old Lie: *Dulce et decorum est/Pro patria mori.*'

Practice questions

1. Choose any poem you have studied which you feel deserves a prize.
   - Name the poem and the poet.
   - Describe what the poem is about.
   - Say why you think it deserves a prize. (2004)

2. Name a poem you have studied which made you feel sad **OR** angry.
   - What was the poem about?
   - Explain how the poet made you feel this sadness or this anger. (2003)

3. Think about poems you have studied. Choose a poem that left a clear picture in your mind.
   - Name the poem and the poet.
   - Describe the picture it left in your mind.
   - Did you like or dislike the poem?
   - Say why you liked or disliked the poem. (2002)

4. Choose a poem which describes: an event **OR** a place **OR** a person. How does the poet describe the *event*, or the *place*, or the *person*? Did you like the poem? Give a reason for your answer. (2001)

5. Name a poem you have studied where the poet was inspired by any **one** of the following:
   - Something the poet saw.
   - Something the poet felt.
   - Something the poet heard.
   - Something the poet remembered.

   Refer to the poem you have chosen, and say clearly:
   - What the poem was about.
   - How the poet described things.
   - Why you liked or disliked the poem. (2000)

6. From the poems you have studied, choose a poem which dealt with any one of the following topics:
   - People.
   - Animals.

Refer to the poem you chose and say clearly:

- What the poem was about.
- What feelings were conveyed in the poem.
- Why you liked or disliked the poem. (1999)

Chapter 7
Fiction

If this section appears in section 4, then it is compulsory and you must answer the questions on fiction. If it appears in section 5, 6 or 7, you have a choice and only have to answer two of the three sections. Please note that fiction is the section most featured in section 4.

In the fiction section, you are asked to read an extract from a novel and answer the questions that follow. The last question will ask you about the novel or short stories you have studied and you will have to write two or three paragraphs on that novel or short story.

UNSEEN FICTION

There are several types of question asked on the unseen fiction extract.

Comprehension questions

These questions ask if you understood the passage and require you to find information in the extract. In your answers to these questions, it is important that you do the following:

- Always use full sentences.
- Answer **exactly** what the question is asking you. In fact, you should use the wording from the question in your answer to ensure that you are answering the question asked.
- Use quotations from the text to support your answer. Your quotes do not need to be long, just to the point.

Character questions

You will be asked about a character from the text on the paper. You may be asked what type of person you think they are, how they relate to the other characters or how we know something about their personality. Your answer should be based on three things: what the character **does**, what the character **says** and how the writer **describes** the character. In your answer, you should make your point, use the quotation to support it and explain your point. Look at the sample answer on pp. 117–18 to see examples of this.

Atmosphere questions

You may be asked how the writer creates atmosphere or tension in the extract. Writers usually create tension by using very short sentences, by using dialogue or by describing the atmosphere using adjectives (describing words), similes and metaphors. Try to identify the use of any of these techniques in the extract.

Opinion questions

You may be asked your opinion on some aspect of the extract. In your answer, try to be positive. Saying that you don't like the piece because it is boring does not help the examiner to give you marks. Look at the various aspects of the extract and use them as reasons why you like it. The following list may give you some ideas:

- **Characters:** You could say that you liked the central character and how they related to the other characters. Or you could identify with the central character, especially if the writer tells us what is going on in the character's head.
- **Dialogue:** The dialogue is any written, direct speech in the piece. Writers often use dialogue to make the scene seem more realistic and to create tension. You could say you liked the use of dialogue as it made the piece realistic or added tension/humour/suspense to the extract.
- **Descriptive passage:** If the writer describes the scene very well using adjectives (describing words) and similes (comparisons using the words 'like' or 'as'), then you could comment on this aspect of the piece.

Sample question

Read this extract carefully and look at the sample answers that follow.

WALTER'S STORY

1. I was twelve years old when I first succeeded in flying. The man in the black suit who called himself Master Yehudi taught me to do it and I'm not going to pretend I learned the trick overnight. Master Yehudi found me when I was nine, an orphan boy begging on the streets of St Louis, Missouri, USA on a cold Saturday night in November.

   'You're no better than an animal,' he said. 'If you stay where you are, you'll be dead before winter is out. If you come with me, I'll teach you how to fly and we'll both end up millionaires.'

2. These were the first words that Master Yehudi spoke to me and even though many, many years have passed since that night, it's as if I can still hear the words coming from the master's mouth. At first, I thought he was just another Saturday night drunk.

   'Ain't nobody can fly, mister,' I said. 'That's what birds do and I sure as hell ain't no bird. And anyway, why do you need *me*?'

   'Because you're the answer to my prayers, son. That's why I want you. Because you have the gift.'

   'Gift? I ain't got no gift. And anyway, what would you know about it? You only started talking to me a minute ago.'

   'That's where you're wrong,' he continued. 'I've been watching you for a week. I even had a long conversation with your Uncle Slim and your Aunt Peg this morning. Your uncle is sure a nice piece of work. He's willing to let you go without a penny changing hands. Imagine that, boy. I didn't even have to pay for you!'

3. I suddenly realised that this was not just another Saturday night drunk and when Master Yehudi sprang the news on me that my aunt and uncle wanted to be rid of me, I felt as if I had been punched in the face. I was

tough for my age and even though Aunt Peg and Uncle Slim weren't much, they were the only family I'd got and it was this that made me ready for anything – even a crazy thing like vanishing into the night with a stranger.

4. 'Okay, mister,' I said, dropping my voice and giving him my best cut-throat stare, 'you've got yourself a deal. But you'd better come through with what you say. I might be small, but I never let a man forget a promise.'

Source: Adapted for the 2005 exam paper from *Mr Vertigo* by Paul Auster

Questions

A. (i)   Where did Walter first meet Master Yehudi?   (5)
    (ii) What did Master Yehudi promise Walter?   (5)
    (iii) Why did Master Yehudi pick out Walter?   (5)
    (iv) What agreement did Master Yehudi make with Walter's
          Uncle Slim?   (5)

B. 'I suddenly realised that this was not just another Saturday night drunk.'
    What made Walter realise this?   (10)

C. Walter tells us that he was 'tough'. (paragraph 3) Would you agree with
    his opinion of himself? Give reasons for your answer.   (10)

Sample answer

A. (i)   *Where did Walter first meet Master Yehudi?*   (5)
          Walter first met Master Yehudi on the streets of St Louis, Missouri,
          USA on a cold Saturday night in November.

    (ii) *What did Master Yehudi promise Walter?*   (5)
          Master Yehudi promised Walter that he would teach him how
          to fly and that they would both end up millionaires.

    (iii) *Why did Master Yehudi pick out Walter?*   (5)
          Master Yehudi picked out Walter because he said he had the gift.

(iv) *What agreement did Master Yehudi make with Walter's Uncle Slim?*   (5)
Master Yehudi made an agreement with Walter's Uncle Slim to take Walter without a penny changing hands.

B.   *'I suddenly realised that this was not just another Saturday night drunk.'*
What made Walter realise this?   (10)
Walter realised this was not just another Saturday night drunk when Master Yehudi said that he had been watching him for a week and that he had had a long conversation with his Uncle Slim and Aunt Peg that morning and that they 'wanted to be rid of' him.

C.   *Walter tells us that he was 'tough'. (paragraph 3) Would you agree with his*
opinion of himself? Give reasons for your answer.   (10)
I think Walter was tough because he was out begging on the streets on a cold Saturday night in November and he stands up to Master Yehudi when he says, 'I might be small, but I never let a man forget a promise.' This shows us that he is quite tough for a nine-year-old.

But I also feel that Walter is not as tough as he thinks he is, as when he hears that his aunt and uncle don't want him any more, he felt as if he 'had been punched in the face'. This shows us that he is hurt by their actions and not as tough as he thinks.

Exam hints

- Note that the answers in question A use the wording of the question and full sentences.
- Note in answer C each paragraph contains a point, a quote to support it and an explanation.

Read the following extract and answer the questions that follow.

THANK YOU MA'AM

1. She was a large woman with a large handbag that had everything in it but a hammer and nails. It had a long strap, and she carried it slung across her shoulder. It was about eleven o'clock at night, dark, and she was walking alone, when a boy ran up behind her and tried to snatch her handbag. The strap broke and he lost his balance, fell on his back on the sidewalk and his

legs flew up. The large woman simply turned around. She reached down, picked the boy up by his shirt front, and shook him until his teeth rattled.

2. After that the woman said, 'Pick up my handbag, boy, and give it here.'

She still held him tightly. Then she said, 'Now ain't you ashamed of yourself?'

Firmly gripped by his shirt front, the boy said, 'Yes'm.'

The woman said, 'What did you want to do it for?'

'Lady, I'm sorry,' whispered the boy.

'Um-hum! Your face is dirty. I got a great mind to wash your face for you. Ain't you got nobody at home to tell you to wash your face?'

'No'm,' said the boy.

'Then it will get washed this evening,' said the large woman, starting up the street, dragging the frightened boy behind her.

3. The boy looked as if he were fourteen or fifteen, frail and willow-wild, in tennis shoes and blue jeans. The woman said, 'You ought to be my son. I would teach you right from wrong. Least I can do right now is to wash your face. Are you hungry?'

'No'm,' said the being-dragged boy. 'I just want you to turn me loose.'

'When I get through with you, sir,' the large woman said, 'you are going to remember Mrs. Luella Bates Washington Jones.'

4. Sweat popped out on the boy's face and he began to struggle. Mrs. Jones stopped, jerked him around in front of her and continued to drag him up the street. When she got to her door, she dragged the boy inside and into a large room at the rear of the house.

She said, 'What is your name?'

'Roger,' answered the boy.

'Then, Roger, you go to that sink and wash your face,' said the woman, whereupon she turned him loose – at last. Roger looked at the door – looked at the woman – looked at the door – and went to the sink.

5. 'Let the water run until it gets warm,' she said. 'Here's a clean towel.'

'You gonna take me to jail?' asked the boy, bending over the sink.

'Not with that face, I would not take you nowhere,' said the woman. 'Here I am trying to get home to cook me a bite to eat, and you snatch my handbag! Maybe you ain't been to your supper either, late as it be. Have you?'

'There's nobody home at my house,' said the boy.

'Then we'll eat,' said the woman. 'I believe you're hungry – or been hungry – to try to snatch my handbag!'

Source: Adapted for the 2004 exam paper from 'Thank You Ma'am' by
Langston Hughes

Questions

A.   What hints do you find throughout this passage that Mrs Jones was indeed 'a large woman'?   (10)

B.   What evidence do we have that Roger is not well cared for at home? (10)

C.   Our impression of Mrs Jones changes as we read this extract. How does she change?   (10)

D.   Roger has the opportunity to escape – but he doesn't. Why do you think he doesn't?   (10)

STUDIED FICTION

In the last question in the fiction section you are asked about the novel or short story you have studied. Each year the question varies, but essentially there are several things you need to be able to write about concerning your novel or short story.

Character

You need to be able to discuss one or more characters from your novel or short story. You also must be able to discuss how they changed in the novel and what caused that change. How did the main character relate to other characters in the book? Why did you find the main character interesting?

Key moments

You need to be able to identify the key moments in the novel or short story, describe them and say why they are important.

Relationships

You need to be able to describe a central relationship in the novel or short story. What is the relationship like at the beginning of the story? How does it change in the middle of the story? What causes that change? At the end of the story, how are things different?

Beginning/end of the story

How does the story begin? Does the writer use a description of a scene or does he jump straight in with dialogue? How are the main characters introduced? At the end of the novel, how is the plot resolved? Does everything end happily for all the characters?

Opinion

You should have formed an opinion of the story. Try to be positive – focus on the good parts of the story and think about the parts of it that you particularly enjoyed. You may be asked what you thought of the story or to write a review of the story, so try to be balanced in your opinion.

The following short stories may be useful to you in answering the exam questions.

THE SNIPER
by Liam O'Flaherty

The long June twilight faded into night. Dublin lay enveloped in darkness but for the dim light of the moon that shone through fleecy clouds, casting a pale light as of approaching dawn over the streets and the dark waters of the Liffey. Around the beleaguered Four Courts the heavy guns roared. Here and there through the city, machine guns and rifles broke the silence of the night, spasmodically, like dogs barking on lone farms. Republicans and Free Staters were waging civil war

On a rooftop near O'Connell Bridge, a Republican sniper lay watching. Beside him lay his rifle and over his shoulders was slung a pair of field glasses. His face was the face of a student, thin and ascetic, but his eyes had the cold gleam of the fanatic. They were deep and thoughtful, the eyes of a man who is used to looking at death.

He was eating a sandwich hungrily. He had eaten nothing since morning. He had been too excited to eat. He finished the sandwich, and, taking a flask of whiskey from his pocket, he took a short drought. Then he returned the flask to his pocket. He paused for a moment, considering whether he should risk a smoke. It was dangerous. The flash might be seen in the darkness, and there were enemies watching. He decided to take the risk.

Placing a cigarette between his lips, he struck a match, inhaled the smoke hurriedly and put out the light. Almost immediately, a bullet flattened itself against the parapet of the roof. The sniper took another whiff and put out the cigarette. Then he swore softly and crawled away to the left.

Cautiously he raised himself and peered over the parapet. There was a flash and a bullet whizzed over his head. He dropped immediately. He had seen the flash. It came from the opposite side of the street.

He rolled over the roof to a chimney stack in the rear, and slowly drew himself up behind it, until his eyes were level with the top of the parapet. There was nothing to be seen – just the dim outline of the opposite housetop against the blue sky. His enemy was under cover.

Just then an armoured car came across the bridge and advanced slowly up the street. It stopped on the opposite side of the street, fifty yards ahead. The sniper could hear the dull panting of the motor. His heart beat faster. It was an enemy car. He wanted to fire, but he knew it was useless. His bullets would never pierce the steel that covered the grey monster.

Then round the corner of a side street came an old woman, her head covered by a tattered shawl. She began to talk to the man in the turret of the car. She was pointing to the roof where the sniper lay. An informer.

The turret opened. A man's head and shoulders appeared, looking toward the sniper. The sniper raised his rifle and fired. The head fell heavily on the turret wall. The woman darted toward the side street. The sniper fired again. The woman whirled round and fell with a shriek into the gutter.

Suddenly from the opposite roof a shot rang out and the sniper dropped his rifle with a curse. The rifle clattered to the roof. The sniper thought the noise would wake the dead. He stooped to pick the rifle up. He couldn't lift it. His forearm was dead. 'I'm hit,' he muttered.

Dropping flat onto the roof, he crawled back to the parapet. With his left hand he felt the injured right forearm. The blood was oozing through the sleeve of his coat. There was no pain – just a deadened sensation, as if the arm had been cut off.

Quickly he drew his knife from his pocket, opened it on the breastwork of the parapet, and ripped open the sleeve. There was a small hole where the bullet had entered. On the other side there was no hole. The bullet had lodged in the bone. It must have fractured it. He bent the arm below the wound. The arm bent back easily. He ground his teeth to overcome the pain.

Then taking out his field dressing, he ripped open the packet with his knife. He broke the neck of the iodine bottle and let the bitter fluid drip into the wound. A paroxysm of pain swept through him. He placed the cotton wadding over the wound and wrapped the dressing over it. He tied the ends with his teeth.

Then he lay still against the parapet, and, closing his eyes, he made an effort of will to overcome the pain.

In the street beneath all was still. The armoured car had retired speedily over the bridge, with the machine gunner's head hanging lifeless over the turret. The woman's corpse lay still in the gutter

The sniper lay still for a long time nursing his wounded arm and planning escape. Morning must not find him wounded on the roof. The enemy on the opposite roof covered his escape. He must kill that enemy and he could not use his rifle. He had only a revolver to do it. Then he thought of a plan.

Taking off his cap, he placed it over the muzzle of his rifle. Then he pushed the rifle slowly upward over the parapet, until the cap was visible from the opposite side of the street. Almost immediately there was a report, and a bullet pierced the centre of the cap. The sniper slanted the rifle forward. The cap slipped down into the street. Then catching the rifle in the middle, the sniper dropped his left hand over the roof and let it hang, lifelessly. After a few moments he let the rifle drop to the street. Then he sank to the roof, dragging his hand with him.

Crawling quickly to his feet, he peered up at the corner of the roof. His ruse had succeeded. The other sniper, seeing the cap and rifle fall, thought that he had killed his man. He was now standing before a row of chimney pots, looking across, with his head clearly silhouetted against the western sky.

The Republican sniper smiled and lifted his revolver above the edge of the parapet. The distance was about fifty yards – a hard shot in the dim light, and his right arm was paining him like a thousand devils. He took a steady aim. His hand trembled with eagerness. Pressing his lips together, he took a deep breath through his nostrils and fired. He was almost deafened with the report and his arm shook with the recoil.

Then when the smoke cleared, he peered across and uttered a cry of joy. His enemy had been hit. He was reeling over the parapet in his death agony. He struggled to keep his feet, but he was slowly falling forward as if in a dream. The rifle fell from his grasp, hit the parapet, fell over, bounded off the pole of a barber's shop beneath and then clattered on the pavement.

Then the dying man on the roof crumpled up and fell forward. The body turned over and over in space and hit the ground with a dull thud. Then it lay still.

The sniper looked at his enemy falling and he shuddered. The lust of battle died in him. He became bitten by remorse. The sweat stood out in beads on his forehead. Weakened by his wound and the long summer day of fasting and watching on the roof, he revolted from the sight of the shattered mass of his dead enemy. His teeth chattered, he began to gibber to himself, cursing the war, cursing himself, cursing everybody.

He looked at the smoking revolver in his hand, and with an oath he hurled it to the roof at his feet. The revolver went off with a concussion and the bullet whizzed past the sniper's head. He was frightened back to his senses by the shock. His nerves steadied. The cloud of fear scattered from his mind and he laughed.

Taking the whiskey flask from his pocket, he emptied it a drought. He felt reckless under the influence of the spirit. He decided to leave the roof now and look for his company commander, to report. Everywhere around was quiet. There was not much danger in going through the streets. He picked up his revolver and put it in his pocket. Then he crawled down through the skylight to the house underneath.

When the sniper reached the laneway on the street level, he felt a sudden curiosity as to the identity of the enemy sniper whom he had killed. He decided that he was a good shot, whoever he was. He wondered did he know him. Perhaps he had been in his own company before the split in the army.

He decided to risk going over to have a look at him. He peered around the corner into O'Connell Street. In the upper part of the street there was heavy firing, but around here all was quiet.

The sniper darted across the street. A machine gun tore up the ground around him with a hail of bullets, but he escaped. He threw himself face downward beside the corpse. The machine gun stopped.

Then the sniper turned over the dead body and looked into his brother's face.

Questions

1. How does the writer set the scene of the story?
2. What do we learn about the character of the sniper? What does he do or say that gives you this impression of him?
3. How does the rivalry between the two snipers develop?
4. What is your opinion of the end of the story?

FIRST CONFESSION
by Frank O'Connor

All the trouble began when my grandfather died and my grandmother – my father's mother – came to live with us. Relations in the one house are a strain at the best of times, but, to make matters worse, my grandmother was a real old countrywoman and quite unsuited to the life in town. She had a fat, wrinkled old face, and, to Mother's great indignation, went round the house in bare feet – the boots had her crippled, she said. For dinner she had a jug of porter and a pot of potatoes with – sometimes – a bit of salt fish, and she poured out the potatoes on the table and ate them slowly, with great relish, using her fingers by way of a fork.

Now, girls are supposed to be fastidious, but I was the one who suffered most from this. Nora, my sister, just sucked up to the old woman for the penny she got every Friday out of the old-age pension, a thing I could not do. I was too honest, that was my trouble; and when I was playing with Bill Connell, the sergeant-major's son, and saw my grandmother steering up the path with the jug of porter sticking out from beneath her shawl, I was mortified. I made excuses not to let him come into the house, because I could never be sure what she would be up to when we went in.

When Mother was at work and my grandmother made the dinner I wouldn't touch it. Nora once tried to make me, but I hid under the table from her and took the bread-knife with me for protection. Nora let on to be very indignant (she wasn't, of course, but she knew Mother saw through her, so she sided with Gran) and came after me. I lashed out at her with the bread-knife, and after that she left me alone. I stayed there till Mother came in from work and made my dinner, but when Father came in later, Nora said in a shocked voice: 'Oh, Dadda, do you know what Jackie did at dinnertime?' Then, of course, it all came out; Father gave me a flaking; Mother interfered, and for days after that he didn't speak to me and Mother barely spoke to Nora.

And all because of that old woman! God knows, I was heart-scalded. Then, to crown my misfortunes, I had to make my first confession and communion. It was an old woman called Ryan who prepared us for these. She was about the one age with Gran; she was well-to-do, lived in a big house on Montenotte, wore a black cloak and bonnet, and came every day to school at three o'clock when we should have been going home, and talked to us of hell. She may have mentioned the other place as well, but that could only have been by accident, for hell had the first place in her heart.

She lit a candle, took out a new half-crown, and offered it to the first boy who would hold one finger – only one finger! – in the flame for five minutes by the school clock. Being always very ambitious I was tempted to volunteer, but I thought it might look greedy. Then she asked were we afraid of holding one finger – only one finger! – in a little candle flame for five minutes and not afraid of burning all over in roasting hot furnaces for all eternity. 'All eternity! Just think of that! A whole lifetime goes by and it's nothing, not even a drop in the ocean of your sufferings.' The woman was really interesting about hell, but my attention was all fixed on the half-crown. At the end of the lesson she put it back in her purse. It was a great disappointment; a religious woman like that, you wouldn't think she'd bother about a thing like a half-crown.

Another day she said she knew a priest who woke one night to find a fellow he didn't recognise leaning over the end of his bed. The priest was a bit frightened, naturally enough, but he asked the fellow what he wanted, and the fellow said in a deep, husky voice that he wanted to go to confession. The priest said it was an awkward time and wouldn't it do in the morning, but the fellow said that last time he went to confession, there was one sin he kept back, being ashamed to mention it, and now it was always on his mind. Then the priest knew it was a bad case, because the fellow was after making a bad confession and committing a mortal sin. He got up to dress, and just then the cock crew in the yard outside, and lo and behold! – when the priest looked round there was no sign of the fellow, only a smell of burning timber, and when the priest looked at his bed didn't he see the print of two hands burned in it? That was because the fellow had made a bad confession. This story made a shocking impression on me.

But the worst of all was when she showed us how to examine our conscience. Did we take the name of the Lord, our God, in vain? Did we honour our father and our mother? (I asked her did this include grandmothers and she said it did.) Did we love our neighbours as ourselves? Did we covet our neighbour's goods? (I thought of the way I felt about the penny that Nora got every Friday.) I decided that, between one thing and another, I must have broken the whole ten commandments, all on account of that old woman, and so far as I could see, so long as she remained in the house, I had no hope of ever doing anything else.

I was scared to death of confession. The day the whole class went, I let on to have a toothache, hoping my absence wouldn't be noticed, but at three o'clock, just as I was feeling safe, along comes a chap with a message from Mrs Ryan that I was to go to confession myself on Saturday and be at the chapel for communion with the rest. To make it worse, Mother couldn't come with me and sent Nora instead.

Now, that girl had ways of tormenting me that Mother never knew of. She held my hand as we went down the hill, smiling sadly and saying how sorry she was for me, as if she were bringing me to the hospital for an operation.

'Oh, God help us!' she moaned. 'Isn't it a terrible pity you weren't a good boy? Oh, Jackie, my heart bleeds for you! How will you ever think of all your sins? Don't forget you have to tell him about the time you kicked Gran on the shin.'

'Lemme go!' I said, trying to drag myself free of her. 'I don't want to go to confession at all.'

'But sure, you'll have to go to confession, Jackie!' she replied in the same regretful tone. 'Sure, if you didn't, the parish priest would be up to the house, looking for you. 'Tisn't, God knows, that I'm not sorry for you. Do you remember the time you tried to kill me with the bread-knife under the table? And the language you used to me? I don't know what he'll do with you at all, Jackie. He might have to send you up to the bishop.'

I remember thinking bitterly that she didn't know the half of what I had to tell – if I told it. I knew I couldn't tell it, and understood perfectly why the fellow in Mrs Ryan's story made a bad confession; it seemed to me a great shame that people wouldn't stop criticising him. I remember that steep hill down to the church, and the sunlit hillsides beyond the valley of the river, which I saw in the gaps between the houses like Adam's last glimpse of Paradise.

Then, when she had manoeuvred me down the long flight of steps to the chapel yard, Nora suddenly changed her tone. She became the raging malicious devil she really was.

'There you are!' she said with a yelp of triumph, hurling me through the church door. 'And I hope he'll give you the penitential psalms, you dirty little caffler.'

I knew then I was lost, given up to eternal justice. The door with the coloured-glass panels swung shut behind me, the sunlight went out and gave place to deep shadow, and the wind whistled outside so that the silence within seemed to crackle like ice under my feet. Nora sat in front of me by the confession box. There were a couple of old women ahead of her, and then a miserable-looking poor devil came and wedged me in at the other side, so that I couldn't escape even if I had the courage. He joined his hands and rolled his eyes in the direction of the roof, muttering aspirations in an anguished tone, and I wondered had he a grandmother too. Only a grandmother could account for a fellow behaving in that heartbroken way, but he was better off than I, for he at least could go and confess his sins; while I would make a bad confession and then die in the night and be continually coming back and burning people's furniture.

Nora's turn came, and I heard the sound of something slamming, and then her voice as if butter wouldn't melt in her mouth, and then another slam, and out she came. God, the hypocrisy of women! Her eyes were lowered, her head was bowed, and her hands were joined very low down on her stomach, and she walked up the aisle to the side altar looking like a saint. You never saw such an exhibition of devotion; and I remembered the devilish malice with which she had tormented me all the way from our door, and wondered were all religious people like that, really. It was my turn now. With the fear of damnation in my soul I went in, and the confessional door closed of itself behind me. It was pitch-dark and I couldn't see the priest or anything else. Then I really began to be frightened. In the darkness it was a matter between God and me, and He had all the odds. He knew what my intentions were before I even started; I had no chance. All I had ever been told about confession got mixed up in my mind, and I knelt to one wall and said: 'Bless me, father, for I have sinned; this is my first confession.' I waited for a few minutes, but nothing happened, so I tried it on the other wall. Nothing happened there either. He had me spotted all right.

It must have been then that I noticed the shelf at about one height with my head. It was really a place for grown-up people to rest their elbows, but in my distracted state I thought it was probably the place you were supposed to kneel. Of course, it was on the high side and not very deep, but I was always good at climbing and managed to get up all right. Staying up was the trouble. There was room only for my knees, and nothing you could get a grip on but a sort of wooden moulding a bit above it. I held on to the moulding and repeated the words a little louder, and this time something happened all right. A slide was slammed back; a little light entered the box, and a man's voice said, 'Who's there?'

''Tis me, father,' I said for fear he mightn't see me and go away again. I couldn't see him at all. The place the voice came from was under the moulding, about level with my knees, so I took a good grip of the moulding and swung myself down till I saw the astonished face of a young priest looking up at me. He had to put his head on one side to see me, and I had to put mine on one side to see him, so we were more or less talking to one another upside-down. It struck me as a queer way of hearing confessions, but I didn't feel it my place to criticise.

'Bless me, father, for I have sinned; this is my first confession,' I rattled off all in one breath, and swung myself down the least shade more to make it easier for him.

'What are you doing up there?' he shouted in an angry voice, and the strain the politeness was putting on my hold of the moulding, and the shock of being addressed in such an uncivil tone, were too much for me. I lost my grip, tumbled, and hit the door an unmerciful wallop before I found myself flat on my back in the middle of the aisle. The people who had been waiting stood up with their mouths open. The priest opened the door of the middle box and came out, pushing his biretta back from his forehead; he looked something terrible. Then Nora came scampering down the aisle.

'Oh, you dirty little caffler!' she said. 'I might have known you'd do it. I might have known you'd disgrace me. I can't leave you out of my sight for one minute.'

Before I could even get to my feet to defend myself she bent down and gave me a clip across the ear. This reminded me that I was so stunned I had even forgotten to cry, so that people might think I wasn't hurt at all, when in fact I was probably maimed for life. I gave a roar out of me.

'What's all this about?' the priest hissed, getting angrier than ever and pushing Nora off me. 'How dare you hit the child like that, you little vixen?'

'But I can't do my penance with him, father,' Nora cried, cocking an outraged eye up at him.

'Well, go and do it, or I'll give you some more to do,' he said, giving me a hand up. 'Was it coming to confession you were, my poor man?' he asked me.

''Twas, father,' said I with a sob.

'Oh,' he said respectfully, 'a big hefty fellow like you must have terrible sins. Is this your first?'

''Tis, father,' said I.

'Worse and worse,' he said gloomily. 'The crimes of a lifetime. I don't know will I get rid of you at all today. You'd better wait now till I'm finished with these old ones. You can see by the looks of them they haven't much to tell.'

'I will, father,' I said with something approaching joy.

The relief of it was really enormous. Nora stuck out her tongue at me from behind his back, but I couldn't even be bothered retorting. I knew from the very moment that man opened his mouth that he was intelligent above the ordinary. When I had time to think, I saw how right I was. It only stood to reason that a fellow confessing after seven years would have more to tell than people that went every week. The crimes of a lifetime, exactly as he said. It was only what he expected, and the rest was the cackle of old women and girls with their talk of hell, the bishop, and the penitential psalms. That was all they knew. I started to make my examination of conscience, and barring the one bad business of my grandmother, it didn't seem so bad.

The next time, the priest steered me into the confession box himself and left the shutter back, that way I could see him get in and sit down at the further side of the grille from me.

'Well, now,' he said, 'what do they call you?'

'Jackie, father,' said I.

'And what's a-trouble to you, Jackie?'

'Father,' I said, feeling I might as well get it over while I had him in good humour, 'I had it all arranged to kill my grandmother.'

He seemed a bit shaken by that, all right, because he said nothing for quite a while.

'My goodness,' he said at last, 'that'd be a shocking thing to do. What put that into your head?'

'Father,' I said, feeling very sorry for myself, 'she's an awful woman.'

'Is she?' he asked. 'What way is she awful?'

'She takes porter, father,' I said, knowing well from the way Mother talked of it that this was a mortal sin, and hoping it would make the priest take a more favourable view of my case.

'Oh, my!' he said, and I could see he was impressed.

'And snuff, father,' said I.

'That's a bad case, sure enough, Jackie,' he said.

'And she goes round in her bare feet, father,' I went on in a rush of self-pity, 'and she knows I don't like her, and she gives pennies to Nora and none to me, and my Da sides with her and flakes me, and one night I was so heart-scalded I made up my mind I'd have to kill her.'

'And what would you do with the body?' he asked with great interest.

'I was thinking I could chop that up and carry it away in a barrow I have,' I said.

'Begor, Jackie,' he said, 'Do you know you're a terrible child?'

'I know, father,' I said, for I was just thinking the same thing myself. 'I tried to kill Nora too with a bread-knife under the table, only I missed her.'

'Is that the little girl that was beating you just now?' he asked.

''Tis, father.'

'Someone will go for her with a bread-knife one day, and he won't miss her,' he said rather cryptically. 'You must have great courage. Between ourselves, there's a lot of people I'd like to do the same to, but I'd never have the nerve. Hanging is an awful death.'

'Is it, father?' I asked with the deepest interest – I was always very keen on hanging. 'Did you ever see a fellow hanged?'

'Dozens of them,' he said solemnly. 'And they all died roaring.'

'Jay!' I said.

'Oh, a horrible death!' he said with great satisfaction.

'Lots of the fellows I saw killed their grandmothers too, but they all said 'twas never worth it.'

He had me there for a full ten minutes talking, and then walked out the chapel yard with me. I was genuinely sorry to part with him, because he was the most entertaining character I'd ever met in the religious line. Outside, after the shadow of the church, the sunlight was like the roaring of waves on a beach; it dazzled me; and when the frozen silence melted and I heard the screech of trams on the road, my heart soared. I knew now I wouldn't die in the night and come back, leaving marks on my mother's furniture. It would be a great worry to her, and the poor soul had enough.

Nora was sitting on the railing, waiting for me, and she put on a very sour puss when she saw the priest with me. She was mad jealous because a priest had never come out of the church with her.

'Well,' she asked coldly, after he left me, 'what did he give you?'

'Three Hail Marys,' I said.

'Three Hail Marys,' she repeated incredulously. 'You mustn't have told him anything.'

'I told him everything,' I said confidently.

'About Gran and all?'

'About Gran and all.'

(All she wanted was to be able to go home and say I'd made a bad confession.)

'Did you tell him you went for me with the bread-knife?' she asked with a frown.

'I did to be sure.'

'And he only gave you three Hail Marys?'

'That's all.'

She slowly got down from the railing with a baffled air. Clearly, this was beyond her. As we mounted the steps back to the main road, she looked at me suspiciously.

'What are you sucking?' she asked.

'Bullseyes.'

'Was it the priest gave them to you?'

''Twas.'

'Lord God,' she wailed bitterly, 'some people have all the luck! 'Tis no advantage to anybody trying to be good. I might just as well be a sinner like you.'

Source: *My Oedipus Complex and Other Stories*, Penguin.

Questions

1. How does the writer introduce each of the main characters?
2. What is the relationship like between Jackie and Nora at the beginning of the story? Give examples from the story to support your answer.
3. How does the writer describe the scene in the confession box?
4. What do we learn about the character of the priest?
5. How does the relationship between Jackie and Nora change by the end of the story?
6. What do we learn about Jackie's personality throughout the story?
7. What did you think of this story? Give reasons for your answer.

Sample question

Name a novel or short story you have studied in which the writer describes one of the following:

- An interesting character.
- The achievement of something that seemed impossible.
- An adventure.

Describe how the writer tells us about **one** of these events in the novel or short story you have chosen. (2005)

Sample answer

The short story I have chosen is 'First Confession' by Frank O'Connor. In this story he describes the achievement of something that seemed impossible.

In this story a young boy, Jackie, is about to make his first confession but he feels it will be impossible to make a good confession as he will have to tell the priest about his actions towards his sister and his grandmother. His grandmother torments him and gives his sister money but doesn't give him any. His sister also annoys him and he once went for her with a bread knife.

He has heard what will happen to him if he makes a bad confession and he was very scared as he went into the confession box. The writer gives us a very humorous description of his confusion in the confession box. He got so confused about where he was supposed to kneel that he ended up falling out of the box into the aisle of the church.

The priest was very nice to Jackie and put him at ease and listened to all his sins. Jackie told the priest everything and only got three Hail Marys for his penance. His sister Nora was very upset at the end of the story, as Jackie got sweets from the priest.

So by the end of the story Jackie had achieved something that seemed impossible and made a good confession.

Practice questions

1. Name a novel or short story you have studied. Describe briefly your favourite moment in the novel or short story and explain why it is your favourite.

   OR

   Choose your favourite character from this novel or short story and explain why this character is your favourite. (2004)

2. Think about a novel or short story you have studied in which a friendship develops or fails between two people. Say who the people are and why, in your opinion, the friendship developed or failed.

   OR

   You are surprised or upset by the behaviour of one of the characters in a novel or short story you have studied. Explain why such behaviour caused you to be surprised or upset. (2003)

3. Think about a novel or short story you have studied. A storyteller often begins by:
   - Describing a scene, a place or an incident.
   - Introducing a character or two.
   - Writing what the characters say in dialogue.

   Describe the beginning of the story you have studied. Was it a good beginning? Why or why not? (2002)

4. Name a novel or short story you have studied. Describe the most exciting part of the story.

   OR

   Describe the most frightening part of the story.

   How did the writer make that part of the story exciting or frightening? (2001)

Chapter 8
Spelling, Grammar
and Punctuation

Throughout the paper, the examiner will be aware of your standard of writing. This will allow the examiner to reward you for good use of language or penalise you for bad spelling and punctuation.

In order to write well, you don't need to have long involved sentences using lots of big words. You **do** need to make yourself clearly understood. Keep it simple and avoid some basic mistakes. There are a few common mistakes that can be easily avoided. Keeping an eye out for these points will make all the difference.

PUNCTUATION

Punctuation (full stops, commas, apostrophes, etc.) is there for a reason. It is your way of telling the reader exactly what you mean. Sloppy punctuation means that your work will be very difficult to follow and possibly doesn't make sense.

Full stop

The most basic element of punctuation is the full stop.

You must have a full stop at the end of every sentence. A question mark and an exclamation mark have the same function as a full stop. Therefore, every sentence you write should end in a full stop, question mark or exclamation mark.

You can also use a full stop to show that a word has been shortened or abbreviated, e.g. Mr., St.

Capital letters

Every new sentence must begin with a capital letter. Capital letters are also used for the name of something:

- A person's name e.g. James Bond.
- The name of a country or place, e.g. Kildare, Ballyhaunis.
- Books or film titles, e.g. *Mission Impossible*.
- Months and days, e.g. January.
- Rivers, mountains, lakes, e.g. Shannon.
- Sports teams, e.g. Manchester United.

Comma

Commas are used to separate items on a list or to divide phrases in a long sentence. A comma gives the reader an indication where to pause so that the sentence makes sense, e.g. 'I stopped, stared and glanced back again just to be sure.'

Apostrophes

When in doubt, students tend to stick in apostrophes everywhere or else leave them out completely. Either option will leave the examiner trying to guess what you mean, which will result in you losing marks. There are two occasions when you use an apostrophe:

- To show that a letter is missing, e.g. don't = do not, I'm = I am, you've = you have, they're = they are.
- To show ownership, e.g. Mary's dog, the teacher's apple.

Do **not** put an apostrophe before every 's' – it is incorrect and unnecessary!

- If a word is plural (more than one) and has added an 's', e.g. boys, and you wish to show ownership, e.g. the bags belonging to the boys, then the apostrophe goes after the 's', e.g. the boys' bags.
- As with all rules, there is an exception: it is = it's, **but** if you want to show ownership, there is **no** apostrophe, e.g. The horse has lost its shoe.

DIRECT SPEECH

In your personal writing, you will probably use direct speech at some point, e.g. a conversation between two characters.

Follow these punctuation guidelines to write direct speech correctly.

- Start a new line every time a new character speaks. This makes it easier for the examiner to follow who is speaking and makes sure you remember to use quotation marks where necessary.
- The first word in any direct speech is always a capital letter.
- Quotation marks must surround the words that a character says.
- Add a comma before the quotation if it is followed by more writing, e.g. 'Oh hello,' said Mary.

Look at the following sample to see these guidelines at work.

'Why do we have to go today?' whined Jack, Sarah's little brother.

'Because I said so,' said Sarah, 'and I'm in charge.' She walked ahead of him down the street.

'I'm too tired,' he tried again.

'Hurry up or I'll leave you behind!'

Jack rushed to catch up with his sister, but her long strides soon left him struggling behind her.

DIALOGUE

When writing dialogue, you don't need to use quotation marks, but you do still need to use other appropriate punctuation. You may be asked to write a dialogue in the personal writing section or in the drama section of the paper. Look at the following example to see how a dialogue should be written:

Jack: Why do we have to go today?
Sarah: Because I said so and I'm in charge.
Jack: I'm too tired.
Sarah: Hurry up or I'll leave you behind!

Character name and colon:

What they say with full stops/question marks/exclamation marks.

SPELLING

The following points include some of the spelling rules that seem to cause problems and a list of frequently misspelled words.

Plurals

- To create a plural for most words, simply add an 's', e.g. cars, dogs, doors.
- Some words are irregular and form the plural by changing a letter(s) or by staying the same, e.g. children, sheep.
- Words that end in –ch add 'es', e.g. marches, churches.
- Words that end in –o add 'es', e.g. heroes, volcanoes, unless there is a vowel before the 'o', e.g. stereos, videos, **except** pianos, solos, halos.
- Words that end in –y change to –ies, e.g. fly = flies, sky = skies, unless there is a vowel before the 'y', e.g. monkeys.
- Words that end in –x add 'es', e.g. box = boxes.
- Words that end in –f or –fe change to –ves, e.g. loaf = loaves, **except** chiefs, cliffs, roofs.

Other spelling rules

- 'i' before 'e' except after 'c', e.g. thief, receive, **except** eight, either, weird, neighbour, sleigh.
- **There/their/they're:** Learn when to use each of these words, as this is the most common mistake Junior Certificate students make:
  - There = a place or a statement, e.g. 'It's over there', 'There are too many people here.'
  - Their = belonging to them, e.g. their bags, their coats, their hats.
  - They're = they are, e.g. 'They're very tired.'

Frequently misspelled words

Check the following list for words that you frequently spell incorrectly and learn how to spell them.

accept	character	chose	definitely
awkward	choice	conscience	disappointment
beginning	choose	conscious	dissatisfied

except	principal	rough	through
guard	probably	said	tough
naive	psycho	sincerely	vicious
panicked	quiet	skilful	violent
prejudice	quite	thought	

Chapter 9
Exam Papers

JUNIOR CERTIFICATE EXAMINATION, 2006

ENGLISH – ORDINARY LEVEL

360 marks

WEDNESDAY, 7 JUNE — MORNING, 9.30 to 12.00

SECTION 1: READING   [60]

Read this passage carefully and answer the questions which follow it.

"THE HIGHEST PLACE ON EARTH"

Pat Falvey, adventurer and explorer, describes how he felt as he reached the summit of Mount Everest.

1   This was it. The last few metres! I was now about to cross the highest platform on earth. There were thousands of feet of fall-off on all sides, as I walked on this narrow ridge with the world below my feet.

2   A feeling of excitement rose from the pit of my stomach to fill my heaving chest. As I approached the last fifty metres, my emotions were running riot. Those few minutes were the most amazing moments of my life. Step by agonising step I inched my way to the top, stopping every few steps to catch my breath as I took in one of the most amazing views on earth.

3   With about fifty metres to go, something very strange happened to me. I began to feel as if my soul and body had somehow parted company.

Unsure whether I was alive or dead I continued, like a moth attracted to the light of a candle, to make for the summit ahead.

4 Tears of joy streamed from my eyes and froze on my beard as the awesome Himalayan mountains started to unfold below me. The last few aching steps, and there I was, standing on top of the world. I could have roared with joy, but instead I silently prayed. Thoughts of those who had gone before me and, sadly, those who never completed the journey back to Base Camp, ran through my mind.

5 Sharing the moment with my fellow climbers, James and Mike, I just stood there in silence and then turned full circle to take in the greatest view on earth. This was not just another climbing adventure. After years of dreaming, planning, fund-raising, fretting, risk-taking – and, on occasion being more single-minded than was fair to those close to me – I had stepped from dreamland into the bright, sharp light of reality.

6 It was quiet and peaceful as we stood on that patch of sacred ground, six miles high in the sky – no television cameras, no press, and no roaring crowds to distract me. I was excited and elated beyond description. I was so proud to be an Irishman standing on the summit of Mount Everest, the Goddess Mother of the Earth.

Source: *Pat Falvey, "The Quiet Quarter".*
(Adapted)

Find answers to the following:

A. 1 "This was it". (Par. 1) What is the writer, Pat Falvey, referring to in this statement?   (5)

2 "Something very strange happened to me" (Par. 3) What did happen to the writer?   5)

3 Who did Pat Falvey remember as he stood "on top of the world"? (Par. 4)   (5)

4 Describe the writer's feelings as he was standing "on the summit of Mount Everest". (Par. 6)   (5)

B. From your reading of the passage, give *two* reasons why climbing Mount Everest is a very exciting adventure.   (10)

C. Explain the following in your own words:

1 My emotions were running riot. (paragraph 2)   (5)

2 Being more single-minded than was fair to those close to me. (paragraph 5)   (5)

D.	In paragraph 5, Pat Falvey tells us that he had stepped "from dreamland into … reality". What was the dream? What was the reality?	(10)

E.	You are planning a T.V. interview with Pat Falvey and his partners, James and Mike. Write *five* of the most interesting questions you plan to ask them.	(10)

# SECTION 2: PERSONAL WRITING	[60]

Write a composition on **ONE** of the following topics.

> PICK ONLY **ONE** TOPIC

A.	Things that really annoy me. . .

B.	In five years' time. . .

C.	The view from the top.

D.	My computer.

E.	Write a story which at some point includes the sentence: "You have no messages."

F.	According to a 2006 survey, children nowadays prefer gadgets to pets. Imagine that you are one of the pets on page 4 of paper X (see p. 154). Write about your reasons for leaving home.

G.	Winter.

H.	The greatest challenge I have ever faced.

SECTION 3: FUNCTIONAL WRITING [60]

Answer **ONE** of the following, **EITHER A OR B**.

PICK ONLY **ONE** TOPIC

A. Write a letter inviting Pat Falvey (who climbed Mount Everest – see Section 1, READING) to give a talk to the students in your school.
You should include in your letter
- when you would like Mr Falvey to come
- why you have chosen him.

OR

B. **FOR OR AGAINST**
You have been chosen as a member of the Class Debating Team. The motion for debate is:
People today are rude and inconsiderate.
You need to
- decide whether you are **for** or **against** the motion
- think about the points you are going to make
- plan the order in which you will make them.
Now write your SPEECH in full.

SECTION 4: POETRY [60]

Read this poem and then answer the questions which follow:

Life Story

1   When I was a child
I played by myself in a
corner of the schoolyard
all alone.

2   I hated dolls and I
hated games, animals were
not friendly and birds
flew away.

3   If anyone was looking
for me I hid behind a
tree and cried out,
"Go away!"

4   And here I am, the
centre of all beauty
writing these poems.
Imagine!

Frank O'Hara
(Adapted)

A.   What words or phrases throughout the poem suggest that the child was isolated or unpopular? Explain why you have chosen these words or phrases. (10)

B.   Who do you think was responsible for the child being alone? The child? Other children? Adults? Give reasons for your answer. (10)

C.   Does the final stanza of the poem surprise you? Why? Why not? (10)

D.   Would you like to have this child as your friend? Why? Why not? (10)

E.   Think about poems you have studied and choose one which best describes a young person who is *either* happy *or* sad.
   • Name the poem and the poet. (5)
   • Describe the sad picture or the happy picture of the young person in the poem. (5)
   • How does the poet give the impression of sadness or happiness? (5)
   • Say why you liked or disliked the poem you have chosen. (5)

> # YOU MUST ANSWER ANY TWO OF THE FOLLOWING SECTIONS 5, 6, AND 7.

SECTION 5: FICTION   [60]

Read this extract carefully and answer the questions which follow it.

SWALK

The card he was expecting arrived a day early. Mossie Quayle found it waiting for him when he got home from school on 13th February. His first impulse was to chuck it on the fire, for he had no time for this slushy, lovey-dovey St Valentine's Day nonsense; but he didn't do that. Perhaps the sheer size of the white envelope appealed to his sense of curiosity.

"Who's your admirer, then?" his mother asked slyly.

"Some twit of a girl," he said, heading quickly for the privacy of his own room.

Actually, he had a pretty good idea who was torturing him in this way. In yesterday's French class Mary Barrett and Anne Clarke had informed him that he would be receiving a valentine card on the 14th February, adding that this card would have the French word for 'love' on it. *L'amour*, they said, shoving out their lips at him and kissing thin air until Anne Clarke laughed like a camel.

In the peace and quiet of his own room Mossie examined the uninvited card. One of the giant red hearts on the front had a jagged split running through it. It sickened him, that broken heart. Your heart was a thumping big muscle in the middle of your chest, it couldn't snap in two like a cheese and onion crisp. 'My heart longs for you', said one of the lines inside. Hearts couldn't long for anything, they were for pumping blood. 'My brain longs for you' would be better. Not that he wanted the brain of Anne Clarke to long for him or that of Mary Barrett but at least it would make sense from a biological point of view.

On the reverse side of the envelope Mossie noticed a word he had never seen before. It didn't even look English. S W A L K. What did that mean? Was it yet more French? Mossie shoved the whole bundle of rubbish between the pages of an atlas.

Next day in French class he put up his hand and asked quietly: "Miss Ward is 'swalk' a French word?"

"What?"

"The word 'swalk' Miss, is it French?"

"Spell it."

"S-W-A-L-K."

Some tittering from behind made him wonder whether he had asked an intelligent question.

"Are you trying to be funny, Mossie Quayle?" said Miss Ward icily, and then went on to describe the peculiar habits of some French verb, leaving unsolved the mystery of 'swalk'.

When he got home, he immediately asked his mother; "What does 'swalk' actually mean?"

"Sealed with a loving kiss."

"Cut out the goo talk, Ma."

"It does. Goo talk, indeed! S for sealed, W for with, A for a, L for loving, K for kiss. It's short for sealed with a loving kiss."

Hell! And he'd asked Miss Ward if it was French. She'd think he was a fool. Sealed with a loving kiss! Oh, the shame of it. The humiliation he felt was colossal – his pride all drained away.

"I'll get my own back!" Mossie raved. "I'll send them some card, all right, and it won't be sealed with a loving kiss . . ."

– Adapted from **SWALK: Collection of Short Stories by Sam McBratney.**

A.   **1**   Why didn't Mossie throw the Valentine card into the fire immediately? (5)

      2   Why, in Mossie's view, could hearts not be broken? (5)

B.   What did Mossie think of Valentine cards? Support your answer with reference to the text. (10)

C.   From your reading of this passage, what sort of boy do you think Mossie is? (10)

D.   Choose the paragraph in the text which you like best. Explain why you have chosen this paragraph. (10)

E.	Name a **NOVEL** or **SHORT STORY** you have studied in which a character undergoes a change.

- Describe the character at the beginning of the novel or short story.
- Explain who or what caused the character to change.
- Describe the character at the end.
- Did you prefer the character before or after the change had taken place? Give reasons for your answer.	(20)

# SECTION 6: DRAMA	[60]

Read this scene, adapted from KES, and then answer the questions.

Kes is the story of 15-year-old Billy Casper who trains a kestrel – a bird of prey belonging to the hawk family. Billy lives with his mother and his elder brother, Jud. The following scene is set in Billy's house.

Billy is quietly sitting, reading a book from the library when Jud enters.

JUD (*getting ready to go out for the night*)

What do you want that for, when you can't read?

(*He snatches the book from Billy*).

BILLY Give it me back. Come here.

JUD Falconry? What do you know about falconry?

BILLY A lot because I'm goin' to get a young kestrel and train it.

JUD You couldn't train a flea. Anyhow, where you goin' to get a kestrel from?

BILLY I know a nest.

JUD Where is it?

BILLY I'm not telling.

JUD I said where? (*Pushes Billy's face into cushion and puts his arm up his back.*)

Where?

BILLY Give over Jud, you're breaking my arm.

JUD Where, then?

BILLY Monastery farm. (*Jud lets go.*)

JUD You think you know something about them, don't you?

BILLY I know more about them than you anyway.

JUD You ought to an' all. You nearly live down in them woods. It's a wonder you don't turn into a wild man. (*Jud scratches his armpits and runs round the room imitating a wildman.*) "Billy Casper, wild man of the woods . . . ha, ha!" I ought to have you in a cage, I'd make a fortune.

BILLY I've been watching them for hours this afternoon.

JUD (*laughing*) I'm hoping I'll be watching a bird tonight, but she won't have feathers on.

BILLY You ought to have seen them though Jud, you ought to have seen them dive down.

Mrs Casper enters.

MRS CASPER You're a couple of noisy brats. What you tormenting him for Jud?

JUD I never touched him.

BILLY Not much. He nearly broke my arm, that's all.

MRS CASPER O shut it both of you. Where you going tonight then?

JUD Usual, I suppose (*looking into the mirror*): Some bird's going to be lucky tonight.

(*He goes out*)

MRS CASPER (*to Billy*) What you going to do with yourself tonight love?

BILLY Read my book.

MRS CASPER That's nice. What's it about?

BILLY I'm going to get a young kestrel and train it.

MRS CASPER That's nice. I say, what time is it?

BILLY I've cleaned the bottom shed out ready, an' I've built a little nesting box out of an orange box, 'til …

MRS CASPER Ten to eight. I'm going to be late as usual. Here, there's £5 for you. Go and buy yourself some pop and crisps or something. Ta ra.

BILLY *(reading aloud but hesitantly, struggling with the language).* **The** kestrel is about 12–14 inches long. It lives in many different types of places: mountains and hills, open moors, farmland, suburbs and even city centres on occasions…

Lights fade.

– Adapted from **KES** *by Barry Hines and Allan Stronach.*

A.   What do we learn about Billy's character in this scene?   (10)

B.   Basing your answer on your reading of the scene, write what you
      think Billy would put in his diary entry that night.   (10)

C.   Using evidence from your reading of the scene, describe the
      relationship which Billy and Jud have with their mother.   (10)

D.   Write the dialogue (about 10 lines) which could have taken place
      between the two brothers when Jud returns home several hours later
      that night.   (10)

E.   Name a **PLAY** or **FILM** you have studied in which a disagreement occurs.
      • What caused the disagreement?
      • Was the disagreement settled? Why? Why not?
      • Were you satisfied with the ending? Give reasons for your answer.   (20)

SECTION 7: MEDIA STUDIES   [60]

Examine carefully the advertisements on pages 2 and 3 of Paper **X** (see p. 152 and p. 153). Then, answer the questions.

A.   Which of the two advertisements do you find more eye-catching?
      Give reasons for your answer.   (10)

B.   (1) According to the text in the advertisement on page 152, what
           "kinds of good" come from eating candy?   (5)
      (2) Do these arguments for eating candy convince you? Why?
           Why not?   (5)

C.   Describe one way in which the two advertisements are alike **or** unalike.   (10)

D.   Suggest **two** ways for improving the message in **either** advertisement. You should refer to:
  • texts
  • images.
Give reasons for you answer.   (10)

E.   Write a leaflet for a dentist's waiting room in which you suggest the DO's and the DON'T's of keeping children's teeth healthy.   (20)

JUNIOR CERTIFICATE EXAMINATION, 2006

PAPER X OF ENGLISH – ORDINARY LEVEL

(To be used in answering Sections 2 and 7)

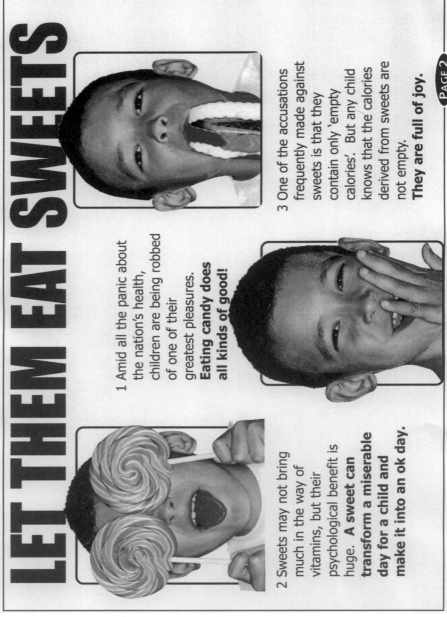

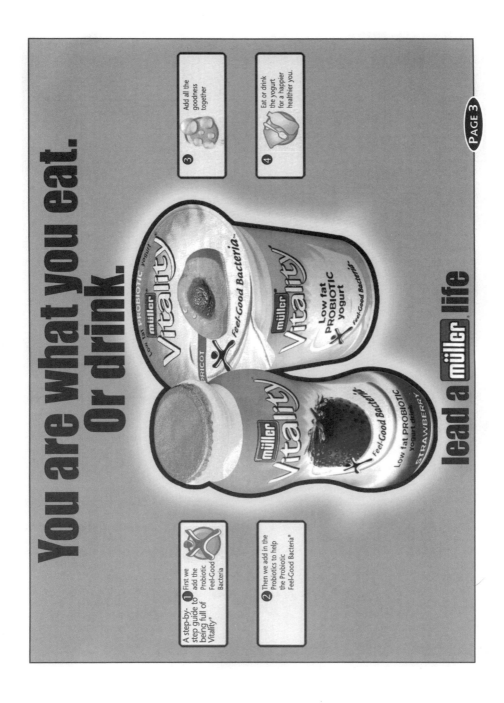

You are what you eat.
Or drink.

A step-by-step guide to being full of Vitality®

1 First we add the Probiotic Feel-Good Bacteria

2 Then we add in the Probiotics to help the Probiotic Feel-Good Bacteria®

3 Add all the goodness together

4 Eat or drink the yogurt for a happier healthier you.

lead a müller. life

PAGE 3

153

The Guardian - 6th August 2005

'They're leaving home...'